Writedown

Lockdown in the Galloway Glens
at the Time of Covid

2020

Copies of *Writedown* have been donated to local archives and libraries. We also feature in the Lockdown Lore Project, run by the Elphinstone Institute at the University of Aberdeen. This is a digital archive of material chronicling Covid-19, which covers the whole of Scotland, available on https://www.abdn.ac.uk/elphinstone/public-engagement/LockdownLore

Printed by J&B Print Ltd., 32A Albert Street, Newton Stewart

ISBN 978-1-9998567-8-6

Contact: Writedown2020@gmail.com
Contributions © the authors
Graphics © Martha Schofield Design

Introduction

When lockdown began, I thought someone ought to record how people here in Galloway were experiencing this unprecedented episode. I had in mind the Government-led Mass Observation project, which created a record of social history during the Second World War through the diaries of thousands of ordinary people.

In anxious times some people turn to writing, and their writing becomes a vital expression of what it is like simply to live through the historical moment. With venues closed I could no longer convene the Glenkens Writers, so I decided to set up a virtual writing group, collectively writing about what it was like to live in, around, or connected to, the Glenkens and wider Galloway in the time of Covid-19.

The Writers

I contacted the Glenkens Writers and other writing groups in Galloway. Through *The Glenkens Gazette* an invitation to join reached every household in the Glenkens. No literary experience was required; participants range from professional writers to those whose expertise lies in completely different fields. Twenty-two people signed up, including three with strong connections here who were exiled by travel restrictions, and one member in Dumfries. All the other contributors live in the Stewartry of Kirkcudbright. Short biographies of the writers appear at the end of the book.

The group is inclusive but not representative. Age and ethnicity reflect our local demographic: many over 70 and all white. As ever, more women than men sign up for writing projects. Those who worked did so from home: key workers didn't have leisure for writing during Covid-19. Two members had to drop out through lockdown-related ill health: one records her life-threatening experience of having Covid-19. Both leave historically significant gaps in the text.

The writers share a strong connection with our local environment, which emerges as a crucial influence on our collective experience. Our connections with Galloway cover a broad spectrum: some contributors were born here, some grew up here, some spent their working lives here; three were farmers. Some raised their children here, some retired here. Like the labourers in the vineyard, we are all here now and part of today's community. Alongside this sense of belonging run strong connections across the world, through family, friends and past careers. Our local is also global.

Several members lived through lockdown in complete isolation. We could only communicate online, but for many the group was a lifeline, its importance frequently reiterated in email exchanges. We have been able to support each other, although no single member knew all the others beforehand. New friendships have been forged, and, with the easing of lockdown, some members are actually meeting for the first time.

The Writing

Everyone has their unique situation, opinion and voice, but as lockdown progresses patterns become apparent, revealing a mosaic of reflections and situations. The overall pattern encompasses a gamut of life experiences, beliefs and affiliations, and yet these very different people express remarkably similar feelings about what is happening to their world.

The book covers the 12 weeks of complete lockdown, starting on Monday March 23rd 2020, the day that Prime Minister Boris Johnson addressed the nation announcing lockdown restrictions, and ending on Monday June 15th 2020, as restrictions were easing. We still have no idea what the future holds, but those 12 weeks gave us more than enough to fill this volume.

For several older people it comes as a shock to find themselves as objects of concern rather than care-givers. For some, ill health takes on new, sinister dimensions. Others struggle with the abrupt cessation of work and income. Perspectives change; small things matter more. There is time to appreciate the unfolding beauty of spring in Galloway, enhanced by astonishingly sunny weather. Isolation, though often hard to bear, brings with it an increased sense of connection with the natural world. At the same time darker themes emerge: responses to Covid-aggravated crises across the world, anxiety about friends and family far away, and increased paranoia and polarisation within communities at home.

The news week by week is the backcloth to our experiences; some events impinge more at the time, some less. A refrain of unease at the disjunction between our lived experience and national and global events appears throughout lockdown. A strong feeling develops of living in two worlds at once; as one reader expresses it: 'my holiday spirit slash boredom and despair'. One reality exists in the moment, relishing small encounters, enjoying the sunshine, embedded in the natural world. The other reality is one of pain, loss and profound dislocation from everything that once seemed normal and kept life in order. The sharpening distinction between inside and outside the bubble - a recurring metaphor throughout - brings out the fragility of 'safe' isolation. Writers begin to look at possible endings that people don't want to speak about, observing how climate change and incompetent political systems are leading us into an unimaginable future. One writer reflects, 'I think that most of us worldwide are quietly grateful for still being here.'

Anxiety deepens as the weeks pass. Writers are weary of restrictions, and at the same time increasingly fearful about how this is going to end. People have given up their civil liberties for the common good, but there are still no solutions to controlling the pandemic, and unease is growing about who is making money out of this, and how or whether personal freedoms will be restored. Questioning of government policy regarding our social and economic future grows more overt; as one writer puts it, 'I can hear the rumbling of capitalism's empty stomach.'

Appalling news continues to come to us: the maternity hospital massacre in Kabul in May, and then in early June the murder of George Floyd in the US, which sparked the Black Lives Matter protests. Some write of their fears for friends and family caught up in terror and violence. This changes what we think, how we experience this changing world. One writer says, 'I can't feel any hope'.

And yet, at the same time, writers have much of their own to celebrate - the first meeting between friends as lockdown eases; the first visit from the grandchildren not seen for three long months; a few freedoms restored; midsummer abundance all around us.

The book ends with the easing of lockdown. The deepening contradictions are in no way resolved. No one knows what will happen next. The story will continue to unfold. Our record had to stop somewhere, although history will not stop. We reach no conclusions, but all twenty-two of us have done our best to tell it like it was.

Margaret Elphistone

June 2020

iv

Acknowledgements

First and foremost thanks go to the twenty-two contributors, *sine qua non.* Their candid, thoughtful, regular reports are the stuff this book is made of.

Very many thanks to our editorial group: Ann Glaister, Carol Salsbury, June Nelson, Mary Smith and Rose Ardron, who brought their expertise and eagle eyes to bear on the diverse contributions to create a coherent text.

We also thank Pat Stonell and Rob Bullock, our external readers, and our readers Frances Hlanze and Ros Elphinstone. Many thanks also to Mike Brown for overseeing production. The project was made possible by being run entirely by volunteers until it went to design and print.

Thanks also to our designer Martha Schofield, and to J&B Print Ltd. in Newton Stewart.

Many thanks to The Glenkens Community & Arts Trust for incorporating the project under its umbrella and for administering the project's finances.

We could not have proceeded without generous grants from The Galloway Glens Landscape Partnership, Oakleaf Camp, The Galloway Association of Glasgow, Local Initiatives in New Galloway, New Galloway Community Council microgrants from Blackcraig Windfarm through Foundation Scotland and a donation from a group member, for all of which we are most grateful.

Margaret Elphinstone

The writers would like to express their thanks and appreciation to Margaret Elphinstone, who conceived and held this project, bringing us together to create a unique record of these challenging times.

March 23rd to March 30th

Boris Johnson announces lockdown...

Millions in first 'Clap for Carers'...

UK fatalities pass 1,000...

Panic buying strips supermarkets...

Frances: **Beginnings**

As events unfolded in Wuhan, my feelings were of horrified fascination. The speed and magnitude were 'over there'. How terrible for them. Did I minimise the possibility of it spreading here?

By the time it had gained ground in Italy, it was on our doorstep. My heart and brain are now both engaged. It will come, but maybe not for a while. Normal life carries on. I fill in at the craft shop on Sunday.

More and more now it is in the UK, and in Africa. There is a looming dark cloud of uncertainty and danger as the news changes from one day to the next. The worst and the best of society are suddenly evident.

On Sunday 15th, I tell Lindi in Nairobi that I think she and Ken would be safer here. Messages flow back and forth. At first, they say no, then quite suddenly they agree. Yes! They consider staying in Lindi's flat in London. Then their next message asks if they can come here. Yes! But Ken is in Nigeria; can he leave there? Can he get a flight? Will he get into Kenya? Will they get flights to UK? He holds two passports, for Cameroon and Spain, which affects his entry rights.

I hear on Monday evening that Ken has successfully boarded in Lagos. Later that evening, Lindi calls from her taxi en route to Nairobi airport, where she will meet Ken. They have a changeover in Qatar. I hear nothing more from them, so an anxious wait until lunchtime Tuesday, when Lindi calls from Gatwick. They will sleep there overnight and arrange a hire car to drive up the next day. Next morning the car hire proves difficult. Lindi's Kenyan address bars her; Ken, however, can do it if he drives all the way to Carlisle, whence they will have to take a taxi. Ken is already exhausted, but they get to Castle Douglas by Wednesday evening. Fortunately, a friend has a holiday home that can be rented for two weeks while they self-isolate. I am so very relieved that they are here. I am full of admiration for their ability to make things happen, to push on through.

That evening, out of the blue, I feel distinctly unwell in a way I can't explain. No cough, no fever. What is it? I cancel my shift in the Castle Douglas shop next day. For the first two days, I feel afraid; I don't know what's wrong, but my body is in some sort of crisis and out of my control. My energy is gone; I sleep and sleep. Maybe I ate something bad? But the frequent sensation of having my chest gripped in a tightening clamp, and disorienting dizziness, make me seek help.

On Friday morning I call the surgery. Within 15 minutes the doctor calls me back, the promptness impressive and reassuring. She diagnoses the virus, prescribes steroids, inhalers and antibiotics. My initial feeling is one of relief. This is what it is. This is what I'm dealing with. Since then I have swung between optimistic visions of recovery, with gardening, painting, making and mending, convivial meals with Lindi and Ken, relishing their presence, and dark wellings-up of fear. There is refuge in sleep, then I wake with a jolt, remembering the situation. For everyone. For me.

A week later, with the benefit of the medication, my symptoms are more under control. My energy comes and goes in wavelets (rather than waves), with much time spent prostrate on the sofa. I wryly observe a pressing of my buttons when friends question whether I have the virus. I can't imagine how fractured families are managing to inhabit confined spaces together. The cracks will engender violence, abuse, fear. How can adolescents be corralled? How can confused elderly be dissuaded from wandering out? And how hideously dreadful and terrifying for people in overcrowded slums, refugee camps or places of conflict.

Meanwhile I read how air pollution levels have dropped since last year. And, of course, air travel has dwindled. There are benefits for the planet.

Rose: **Countdown**

Thursday March 12th: We hesitate to go on a planned weekend to Sheffield. Big things are getting cancelled elsewhere, but it's not alarming enough to put us off.

Friday March 13th: I won't stop at service stations. I make sandwiches and a flask. The roads seem the same, the city as busy as ever.

Saturday March 14th: Our friends are planning a trip to Geneva to visit daughter and grandson. They get a text to say the Swiss government has banned all over-65s from childcare.

Sunday March 15th: The farmers' market is nowhere near as crowded as it usually is. Elbow bumping is the joke we play. I'm glad I've seen old friends. We're making plans to meet again in the months ahead.

Monday March 16th: It's a relief to get back to the village, safe in rural Scotland. Our neighbour comes out with news from the school blog: school play cancelled. Adult helpers not to come in. I take my granddaughter to her swimming lesson. The classes are half-full. It's gone quiet. Oh!

Wednesday March 18th: No helping out at school today and our

3

weekend visitors have cancelled. My life is emptying. Kirkcudbright pool is still open, so I go for a swim; my safe haven. While I'm out I fill up the car just in case. The clothes swap is cancelled; no change of wardrobe this season.

Thursday March 19th: Cairn Chorus is cancelled. The virus has won! I go to town and stock up: a new notebook, a trip to the library, two packs of nicorettes, contact lens fluid. These are my essentials when I'm getting ready to go on a trip. And then, the news we'd been expecting: the schools are closing.

Friday March 20th: Families out in the village to see the kids off on the school bus for the last time. Off they go and I burst into tears. They won't come to our house; no longer the fabric of my life. I still don't see what the point of this is. It's to protect me? The natural order is reversed. I become the vulnerable.

News by text: my friend, Carole, has died of the virus. I was with her in the middle of February. I start paying attention. It's official: I'm 'social distancing'! The community council delivers a newsletter with a sign I can put on the door.

Saturday March 21st: The weather is cold but bright. Spring equinox: my parents' wedding anniversary. I'm glad my mother isn't alive. I don't have to worry about her.

Sunday March 22nd: We're out in the sun, getting manure for the garden. The seeds are ordered, but our wine order won't be delivered. The avalanche is gaining speed.

Monday March 23rd: Lockdown.

Totalitarianism: I understand it now. The safety of certainty. I will do what I'm told. I rely on structure to get me out of bed in the morning. The things I should be doing were always lined up in my mind: cutting short the present moment because the next one is coming along. Now I have all the time in the world and I don't know what to do with it.

Never mind the lack of online delivery slots, I think of women and children locked into abusive homes, people trapped in Syria, Calais,

Lesbos. What will have happened to them when we come out the other side?

We sit on our decking drinking coffee in the Galloway sun. The wood lorries still roll. White vans hurry past.

Look, here comes the bus!

Christine: **Splendid Isolation**

When I first heard about the 'splendid isolation' we were destined for I was very upset. I could put it in much stronger language, but I am too polite! Ever the actress manqué I recalled the famous speech from George Bernard Shaw's *St. Joan* which begins, 'Perpetual imprisonment!' It goes on, 'to shut me from the light of the sky and the sight of the fields and flowers …if only I could still hear the wind in the trees.' After I had recited it I was in a calmer frame of mind.

I phoned the rector of St Margaret's and commiserated with her on her unfortunate start in New Galloway. After all, a heart attack and a closed church is no picnic! She was quite upbeat about it, really cheered me up, and said that she thought that there should be a party afterwards for everyone who had been in seclusion, to celebrate the freedom which we had all missed.

Margaret: **Early Days**

This lockdown looks, in certain lights, like an idyll. An idyll in which people are dying? In which others are immured indoors, children unable to play, adults driven to desperation, homeless people living in terror? Communities without medical services, without basic sanitation or clean water, waiting for the plague to arrive? What kind of idyll is that? No one knows what the future holds. But here, in this garden, I find peace.

I have prepared beds, moved compost, sowed seeds. We're making a new potato bed. Our family has increased by four chickens. Every day I take the dogs for a walk in hidden woods where I never meet a soul. The trees are full of birdsong. Here, where I sit in the garden, sparrows are nesting in the tit-box six feet away. They're quite untroubled by my presence. The male is sitting on the perch outside the door, cheeping loudly.

There is hardly any traffic. Sometimes I hear voices, louder than usual as people call one another from their gardens, keeping the statutory two metres apart. Next door a brother and sister, who haven't played together much recently, are involved in some elaborate noisy game. My own grandchildren sometimes come with their parents bringing deliveries. We wave from a distance. At least I can see them.

Every day I make two phone calls to family and friends, particularly those who are now isolated. Last night I chatted to my cousin Shirley, who can make direct comparisons with the Phoney War. "No," she answers my question, "it wasn't like this at all. But it must have been terrible for the grown-ups." We agreed that time seems to have changed. "I've just been sitting in the sun all afternoon," she says, "yet the day has flown by. The neighbours have been so kind."

Mike shows the grandchildren how to communicate online using naval signal flags. I have a message on my desk: one yellow flag with a black spot in the middle, and one divided diagonally, red top right, yellow bottom left. It means: "You should NOT come too close".

There are no planes in the sky. The air is clear, even in Beijing: I saw it on the news. How long have we campaigned for this? The suffragettes got the vote not because of their protests (though these prepared the way) but because of the cataclysm of the First World War. Surely, now we're forced to do things differently, we won't return to the suicidal path of environmental destruction and global expansion? I've lived in hope all my life, but it was beginning to wear thin. The only certainty about what happens next is that it will surprise us. I want to meet you face to face, dear Reader, and ask what you think, but you should NOT come too close.

Gordon: **Having a Rough Time**

My lockdown started early, on February 18th, running on the Southern Upland Way in rain and mud. Little streams trickling over the path. Splat! Ouch! Can't get up! This has never happened before. I've fallen many times but this time there's a broken leg! Call my wife, slither down to the road on my backside. Oh! The puddles are cold.

Doctor, A&E, X-ray, plaster, home, called back following day. As I'm a runner, Eiffel Tower fitted into leg, home, much restricted movement.

So, what to do? I'll resume writing a long dystopian novel I've had on the stocks for years. Some flu-like Crown virus thing which I ignore works its way up the news bulletins. But, what's all this about 70+ people restrictions? That's me and my wife! Never mind, get on, days fly by, words fly on to pages and then it's review, re-read, check dates, read again, putting into practice the things learned from tutors. Quite independently of events, well before this virus hit the news, I'd put a coronavirus-type episode in my book, using a resistant strain of TB instead. It'll be interesting to see how much my book matches real life.

Two shop staff self-isolate and suddenly the New Galloway shop is reduced to two hours a day with people queuing outside so that the six-foot rule is obeyed. The shop keeps its stock up and the suppliers seem to be coping. Empty shelves on the TV. We're very fortunate to have a shop that's managing to keep some service going.

This virus needs to be stopped as soon as possible, but the government is slow to act and then gets it wrong! They cut down trains and buses and then tell people to distance! Pictures of packed tube trains on TV. Stupid! More restrictions declared on March 23rd. This means we won't be able to use the communal walled garden in the Garroch Estate. People will just have to keep it going with minimal presence until we don't know when. Great shame. My planned job there is to clear vegetation and small trees to tidy up and extend the garden car park. Best done before it starts to thicken up in a couple of weeks but that won't be on now.

Oh yes, and no running events this season because of the virus.

June: **A Strange New World**

The virus arrived late in Kirkcudbright. While people in Glasgow and Edinburgh had been living beside it for weeks, in Kirkcudbright Covid-19 was a news item and a scary one. Up there in the cities folk just carried on. Down here places closed, events were postponed, meetings cancelled, sport stopped, the elderly went into hiding, loo rolls flew off the shelves, flour disappeared, shops filled with people and emptied of stuff. And not a case anywhere near.

I drove to Glasgow for a hip operation and couldn't believe the nose-to-tail cars driving into Kirkcudbright at 2 pm on a Tuesday afternoon, along a usually empty road. Local folk seem resentful of these holiday home-owners fleeing the cities. One local shopkeeper told me, "I've lived in my house for 20 years and here are these folk wanting to join things and 'do good'."

I returned from Glasgow, still wearing the old hip, and had my most amusing-ever shopping experience. Places I usually shopped were the ones that still held food: plenty of fruit and vegetables, Greek yoghurt, organic produce, interesting cheese, gluten free. No shortage of anything healthy.

But the situation is promoting camaraderie and some rueful humour. One chap commented that at least there was no shortage of salad. We turned simultaneously and gasped. The large display section usually full of boxes of different mushrooms contained two packs. I took the one with broken pieces of small chestnut mushrooms. The other contained a variety of expensive wild ones. I'm just hoping all this food will be eaten. Are folk panic buying anything they can? Will they then throw most away because they have bought far too much? Some will go rotten, some will pass that ridiculous sell-by date and some they will have no idea how to cook and don't like anyway! Procuring a pack of loo rolls seems to be greeted like a large lottery win. We elderly, quite used as children to using newspaper, are not in the fight. With our make-do-and-mend experiences we are eyeing the leaves and moss.

Beyond doubt there will be a huge increase in obesity; I can see bored people with a stockpile of carbohydrates and sweet things. A search for new activities equals baking and a trillion cupcakes. So no flour in the shops. Domestic abuse and violence will explode, child abuse more so; self-harm and mental health will become huge issues. But kindness, community spirit and self-sacrifice are already surrounding us. I have had so many offers of help.

Beverley: **Care, Kindness and Common Sense**

All the shops closed on Monday! I was going to go to the garden centre on Tuesday to get gro-bags, tomato and cucumber plants and a brush to wash my car with, so telephoned immediately I heard Nicola Sturgeon make the announcement and put in an order just in the nick of time for delivery on Wednesday – their last delivery. I don't understand why the government didn't allow the garden centres and nurseries to stay open just long enough to sell their spring plants. Instead all that precious stock, so lovingly grown and desired by most of us, is to be destroyed and they all risk bankruptcy, unless the government bales them out. What a waste!

I went to the supermarket today at 9 am, the old people's slot. On the way I popped into the garage in Twynholm which has serviced pumps – so much safer - only to find they were closed. I rang the owner, who said he had someone coming in for mower fuel at 12 noon and would that be convenient?

I set off for the supermarket to find about three hundred oldies queuing. As I was shopping for myself and two friends in lockdown, I decided to return tomorrow at 7 am instead. Now having an hour in hand, I thought I would have my daily walk in the Cally woods, so I could return to the petrol station at 12 noon without going all the way home.

There were two cars in the car park, so I parked in the horse car park instead, got out of my car, donned my boots and coat, picked up my trusty stick and set off up the path. A car came down the small road to the Cally Hotel and jammed on its brakes. The driver, who was known to me, opened the window and started shouting abuse and obscenities at me. "Go home, go home, you stupid bloody bitch. I'll call the police!"

"You do that thing," I replied, as calmly as I could, and walked slowly up the path, away from the road. When I was out of sight, I sat down on a rock to try to control my shaking and burst into tears. How dare he? This is my local town wood, I am all alone, there is not a soul to be seen anywhere and I am allowed by the government to exercise for one hour a day.

I hate the sense that anything which smacks of enjoyment seems to be construed as evil. Is this some sort of ancient Scottish Calvinism rearing its ugly head?

Surely the key to surviving this horrible time is care, kindness and common sense.

Cath: **Blessings Counted**

The tables have turned. I've always been the nurturing Mother figure, the wise one (or so I liked to think) to whom everyone came for shelter and sustenance. Now the younger generation are protecting us. I'm not quite old enough for enforced self-isolation, yet our offspring are trying to check (from a distance) that we are complying with the rules and not taking risks – a wacky idea to many of us rebellious baby boomers!

These younger adults are working at home, juggling childcare, education, and assuming responsibility for the oldies – as if they don't have enough to worry about! I offered to look after grandchildren but was firmly told we must stay where we are and look after ourselves.

Our midwife daughter is a front-line NHS worker; babies are born, and their mums need care. Protective clothing was only supplied two days ago. No testing has happened, causing more anxiety in these uncertain times. Our youngest daughter is staying with her sister and family in Airdrie, helping with childcare whilst trying to keep up with her own work and write up her thesis. Her husband has now arrived there safely after getting one of the last flights from Boston. We have no idea how he'll manage to self-isolate in a household of four adults and a toddler!

I wish we all lived in a castle or mansion with enough room for us all to stay together and take care of each other, and yet I count our blessings. We live in a lovely place, with fresh air and birds. I'm not cooped up in a tower block with children driving me insane. I worry about families living 'on the edge' who will tip over into neglect, abuse or violence when faced with endless, shapeless days with bored, restless children.

Having been brought up in the years after the war, we know how to make do with basic staples. Exotic foodstuffs hadn't been dreamt of then: even garlic was a novelty! Now we keep a freezer full of food and a well-stocked larder, but many have neither the resources nor space to do that. We are lucky not to live hand-to-mouth.

We are fine. I feel a bit useless actually, apart from ringing a few more-vulnerable neighbours to check on them. We live pretty normally; miss seeing our friends, going to meetings, films and so on. It was disappointing that our next round of the drama festival had been cancelled, but what's a trip to sunny Greenock compared with a global crisis!

Of course, these endless days need to be filled. There is no excuse now not to do those jobs which we never find time for. I've already cleared two bedrooms, and although I need to be more ruthless in getting rid of things, they are tidier for now.

No need to rush. There is plenty of time.

Leonie: **Wildlife Garden Journal**

My thoughts are slowing down. I have time to notice small things.

> Pioneer of ancient lineage who ventured on to land
> relying on the armour of your segmented carapace,
> left behind your crabby cousins of the seashore,
> found safety in dark places of decomposing leaves.
>
> You emerge at night, slipping in under the door
> like the draught, onto the desert of the kitchen floor
> seven pairs of legs track across the lino to arrive
> on the dry pasture of the carpet where you curl up and die.
>
> Sometimes at dawn, I spot you just in time,
> gently retrieve your fragile form, cup you in my hand
> breathe on you the kiss of life. If I see you move,
> put you back outside where you belong.

Taxonomy
Phylum: Arthropoda. Sub-phylum: Crustacea. Class: Malacostraca
Order: Isopoda. Genus: Oniscus. Species: *Oniscus asellus* - the common
woodlouse, AKA the slater.

Mags: **Alone but Never Lonely**

We live in a bubble: an invisible, dangerous, unknowable bubble. And within that bubble our individual bubbles float around bemused, confused, distancing and helpless.

Saturday is windy and cold. I am at my desk upstairs when my mobile buzzes:

"Mum?"

"Where are you darling?"

"In your shed. It's too windy at the back door."

We both burst out laughing. I make my way carefully down the steep staircase, which has become more and more challenging. She stands at the back door and steps back as I slide it open. A large bag sits on the doorstep bulging with goodies. I know she will have made a special effort to get the things I like.

"Your groceries are in that bag. Take them out and don't touch the bag if you can help it."

"Wow," I think. I wouldn't have thought of being so careful. I take the items out a few at a time and put them on the kitchen worktop. I'll wipe them down with bleach later, as instructed by my lovely health-policing daughter.

She leaves her jacket and bag outside the door and sits in the old rocking chair which I have placed just inside. I retreat across to the farthest corner. She looks tired. Shopping has become quite stressful, she tells me. Waiting in the queue at the supermarket entrance, the person beside her lights a cigarette, but at least he's keeping his distance. Inside, at the checkout, someone texts her: "Don't forget the lemons". Too late. You can't lose your place in that queue.

I want to give her a long hug. I need one too. But mostly I want her to go home and relax with her family. How can I express this without making her feel unneeded, unwanted? I must wipe down the chair after she's gone, she tells me. Her work as a schoolteacher has made her super-cautious. Having mixed with children she may be a carrier, and I am in my mid-seventies, even though I don't feel it. She is my guardian angel. My lovely girl. I need a hug more than I need the groceries. But this is not possible.

Now for the hilarious bit. She needs a pee but doesn't want to use my bathroom. She contemplates going in the garden, but what about the neighbours? Eventually she gives in and I get an audio description as she tries to hover while peeing and not touching anything. It's a palaver, but she is so keen to protect me. We are both giggling when she emerges victorious, having touched nothing. We chat for a while and then she leaves.

How can I watch my daughter through the glass, looking as if she needs the hug I cannot give her? But I am reassured because she lives with her own family where hugs abound.

I take my crutches and go for my daily walk up the road. Half a mile there and half a mile back. Thank goodness for this lovely dry weather.

Sunday is a day of rest so I'll follow the biblical instruction! I rest, read and doze all day. Downstairs my knitting and the jigsaw await my attention, but no, I won't be going there. Chats on the phone break up the day and *BBC Sounds* entertains me with wonderful stories and journalism. Escape into other worlds is possible through words and images. Perhaps being this age is the best age to be while the world outside reels and rocks in disbelief and disaster. Selfish, yes, but I am forbidden to go outside and refuse to feel guilty at not being able to help anyone. But I can put my name on the list, circulated by our community council, for phoning lonely people. I live alone but am never lonely.

Mike: **Prisoners of War**

They did not know when it would end. Or how. Or if they would live to see it. But in the shelters they would sing (we are told) and hug and kiss and whisper in each others' ears. As the bombs fell.

Our roofs are safe today. There is food to be found, one way or another. But the reassuring hand, the impulsive embrace, the spontaneous visit of a friend: all are lost.

Governments on war footing strive to meet our needs. But where is the Ministry of Touch and Caress?

'Isolation', that bleakest of words, may be a tactic of war but not a balm for the soul.

And what a war. All wars have prisoners. But now the prisoners of war are the combatants.

March 30th to April 6th

*Prime Minister in
intensive care...*

*Emergency hospital
at Glasgow's SECC...*

*2,000 confirmed
cases in Scotland...*

*Research reports anxiety
and depression surge...*

Margaret: **Being Here Now**

Spring comes in with an intensity which may be entirely my perception. I come from a world where people devoted much time and money to, as they expressed it, 'living in the present'. Some did courses in mindfulness and meditation. Some went on exotic holidays to far-flung destinations. Some went in for dining out, drink, or possibly illegal drugs or an amazing sex life. Our problem on that other planet was that we believed all rewards lay in the future. The most important goals were also the most distant ones: not tonight's dinner or the next chapter of a book, but the ultimate fulfilment of a dream.

The way off that planet was simply to delete the future. Now I can't take a purposeful journey towards anywhere, so I'm being where I am with a vengeance. Vengeance is maybe the right word. Who gets punished? The people who had already been allocated the worst place. I imagine being stuck in a small flat with a person I'm terrified of. Or having to share my water tap with 500 others, knowing this may kill me. Being told to move on from sunbathing in a park because I have nowhere else to be outdoors. Working from home in the same room as a couple of toddlers who can't understand why they can't go out to play. Having someone I love taken away to die alone. Being taken away myself to die alone.

None of these things is happening to me. Except that it is. Donne said it for me: 'Any man's death diminishes me, because I am involved in mankind, and therefore never send to know for whom the bell tolls; it tolls for thee.'

I think about these things mainly in the evening, when I look at the news. Other times I'm simply here. The blackthorn is out in sheltered places. My peas in their little pots in the greenhouse are beginning to sprout. There are celandines in the hedgerows and kingcups by the burn. I know where the red kites are nesting, and I've seen my first lark. Our hens lay three eggs a day. I gather wild garlic. I throw sticks in the burn for my dog Betty to fetch. Always at the same pools, by the same waterfalls. She is a creature of habit, and I'm learning from her how to be a creature of habit too. Any break in our rhythm is a Serious Event. Monday's Serious Event is the bin men, Wednesday's is our food order, and Friday's is the fish van. That's as far as the future stretches. There is only Now.

Mary: **And So It Begins**

My lockdown began when several events and readings were cancelled. As I cross out six appointments in my diary and look at the empty weeks ahead I feel a surprising sense of lightness at having nothing I need do, no one I need meet. The weather is pleasant and it is easy to get out for our regulation exercise. I am thrilled to be able to photograph both ospreys on their nest. The National Trust volunteers won't be at the platform with their telescopes this year – but I guess there won't be visitors either.

I go to the supermarket to buy a couple of things the DH (Darling Husband – who has been in hunter-gatherer mode for the last few days) didn't get when he did the big shop yesterday. The girl at the checkout is chatty, confessing surprise at how many people have been in the shop this morning. "One man just came for a newspaper," she says. "Not what I'd consider an essential purchase." I feel she gives my bottle of wine an accusing look. "If I didn't have to be here, there's no way I'd come out of my house."

I don't tell her I think a newspaper is definitely an essential item, especially not as she decides I can buy the six onions I have in my basket although, she says, "Technically you are only supposed to have two of any item."

Information and misinformation, updates and analyses come at us so fast I am overwhelmed and limit myself to one news broadcast a day to save my sanity. I need my paper and time to assimilate the news. I think about the numbers being reported – numbers of cases, numbers of deaths. They seem such small numbers – 100 deaths in last 24 hours – but are having such a huge impact on all our lives. We are warned there will be more.

Jawad emails from Kabul. His wife now bakes their bread at home so they don't have to go to the bakery. Thousands of Afghans working in Iran are heading home. He says if Covid-19 only affected poor people in poor countries the West wouldn't be so determined to stop it. He sends a picture of a starving child, captioned: "This 'virus' is called hunger. It kills 8,000 children every day. There is a vaccine. It's called Food." I don't have the courage to put it on Facebook.

If I could ignore the news and my uncomfortable thoughts, I'd be happy. I rather like being a recluse. I'm astonished by the articles everywhere full of suggestions for things to do to prevent boredom during lockdown. Boredom? We surely haven't had time to be bored. I would, though, really like to hug my son.

Katy: **A New Current**

More time is spent online. First with my job, trying to stay in touch with young people. I establish various online groups, join TikTok to make silly videos and research creative resources. Coronavirus updates distract me easily. Our friendship groups make a swift transition to the virtual. None of them choose the same video app or platform. In the space of a few days, I have used Houseparty, Skype, WhatsApp, Facebook, Messenger and Jitsui to talk to friends. We don't usually talk this much. Some are out of work, others are working flat out. But there are silver linings; my friend's Argentinian husband has a short visa extension and my brother moves in with his girlfriend. I'm glad they all get more time together.

My husband has his anaesthetics interview cancelled. They say they are looking into the possibilities of doing this online. We had hoped to find out in April if he had a job and where it would be, but we resign ourselves to not finding out anytime soon.

Although I'm gutted to spend my last few months here distancing myself from a community I love, I don't feel as low as I have done recently. I suppose there's nothing like a global pandemic to put your own problems into perspective. I think back to an article I read once about loss;

the writer couldn't understand how the world carried on as normal after her father had died. I wonder if there's a sense of comfort, especially for those losing loved ones to this virus, that the world is far from normal.

I feel incredibly lucky to still have my job, to be here in Dumfries and Galloway, and to live in a society that has a welfare system. Of course I worry; for our elderly grandparents, my brother whose haven is the remote glens and my sister-in-law who may have to give birth without her partner present. I fear for everyone with the austerity that is sure to follow.

Rose: **Making Do**

I work outside every day trying to hold my world together. I'm getting to know this garden we've inherited. There are brilliant patches of daffodils persisting everywhere. Starry chionodoxa shine out at me. The sounds of a quiet world, making way for bird song. I used to just chuck some seeds in the ground before I went away again. Now I dig, manure, rake and sow with intention. I'm not going anywhere right now.

Taking my turn to cook is an anchor in the day. No longer recipe-led, nipping to the shops for missing ingredients, I look at what we've got, substitute and combine. Goodbye Yotam Ottolenghi; hello greasy yellowed copy of my old friend *The Bean Book*. I make a salad – a tin of lentils from the back of the cupboard, lambs lettuce that I thought was a weed, kale massaged in oil and vinegar as a substitute for spinach, fresh ramsons that I found in the woods.

Rob finds a faded pamphlet – *The Wartime Greenhouse*. This is our folk memory. My mother remembered rationing. As a young bride on a naval base in Cumbria she received care packages of precious flour and sugar from her mother in New York. She told her story of dismay when the week's ration of eggs went to waste in a cake spoiled by adding salt instead of sugar.

It's not as if there is a shortage of food in the shops. Tamsin shops for us. We are keeping safe, doing our bit. I've made a template for our weekly list, preparing for the long haul. We eagerly await her return and check the items off. I hear of queues and arrows on the floor, gaps in the shelves and screens to protect the checkout operators. I am being shielded from a receding outside world and learning about it secondhand. I want to see for myself. I have a wicked thought, to hop on the bus and run away to town without telling anyone. It's just gone past!

June: **Living Alone in Isolation**

It's almost five years since Bryan died, after more than 60 years together. He taught me to love solitude, but now I compromise: an active social life, with folk staying occasionally but a regular return to my peaceful haven. What would isolation be like? So far I'm happy, with sunshine, but it's different. And will I hate grey-wet?

Time becomes strange. A week feels long. Yet each day rushes past. Saturday March 28th, I wake at 6 am with a painful hip. I love being up early. Anything before 8 is free time. But I notice the laundry and checking for rain see it's Sunday and I've lost a day.

On March 19th Covid-19 closed the Golden Jubilee hospital 12 hours before my hip operation; my fourth cancellation. With an aching hip the simplest tasks take forever. And there are many things, abandoned in busier times, to catch up with. Maybe I will point my wall with that sand and cement ordered two years ago. Perhaps I will paint the summerhouse; rationalise the potting shed.

After a week of tottering I decide to try my bike: flat tyres. My neighbour demonstrates the strange pump and, after a dodgy start, friend E and I fly down the estuary. What a relief to be airborne. Then I notice bare canvas among the tread. It's the day before lockdown but the bike shop classes as an essential business. My neighbour fits new tyres.

E mentions the three elderly friends in lockdown moving in together. "Bright idea," I say, "socially, logistically, financially." Next day she suggests we do the same. "No!" I yell. Seeing her face, I add, "We'd be best enemies in days." She agrees. Ai Weiwei says: "I like silence. No sound at all. Maybe I belong to death." That's me - apart from birdsong. I'm visual; could read all day. E would listen all day. And she hates gardening.

What to wear? Gardening, again. Obviously gardening clothes. But then I shall have an hour's cycling. And my neighbouring gardeners have pretty high standards. One has tasteful dungarees with a white blouse. The other, always elegant, wears navy, with matching gloves and a little hat above her midge veil.

Nobody visiting my house. Can the washing-up wait till tomorrow? I hastily tidy my living area after three days' negligence. Must keep some sort of standards.

I have not stockpiled and bought little since the virus. Expecting family for post-op caring, I bought basic supplies. And, as Margaret once said, if you've lived on islands you always have a barrel of flour and one of oats in case the boat can't land.

I could subsist for weeks, but no fruit and vegetables would be hard. I look out at ground elder and dandelions and start rationing the salad: two lettuce leaves, two tomatoes, one radish and a chocolate ginger for afters.

Leonie: **Wildlife Garden Journal**

The volume of bird song has been turned up, the thrush at his post, house sparrows squabbling in the rose bush. Nesting blackbirds furtively enter the bottom of the cypress tree. It is a bit of a giveaway when the well-leafed branches waggle vigorously as they ascend to the nest near the top of the tree.

My best moment was late afternoon, a flight of 21 whooper swans trumpeting and honking, powered overhead across the garden. They were still flying low, having taken off from Loch Ken only a few hundred yards away, and I could hear their beating wings.

I have discovered a seam of gold between house brick and paving. As a child I adored *The Flower Fairies* illustrated by Cicely Mary Barker and the coltsfoot, *Tussilago farfara,* was one of my favourites. I was intrigued by the dark overlapping scales on the stem and the appearance of huge cobwebby leaves long after the flowers.

Roger: **Something Different**

I explore through the screen of trees by the railway to see what I am hearing: a track repair gang at work. I experience the contrast between their purposeful task fulfilment, their uniformed ethos and myself idling by. There's a slight slope after the trees and a metalled path where one can saunter undisturbed by traffic. Even better, there are the colours of the rainbow: fresh flowers decoratively tied to a black iron seat. The seat is the centrepiece of this welcome grass strip. It functions attractively as a rest-the-feet stop, a sit-and-talk opportunity, sometimes collecting dog-walking older local folk like myself. The flowers on the seat are renewed as needed in memory of a departed regular walker and talker, who once enjoyed this alternative to concrete. Her ashes were scattered here.

Today, joyously, something different. I listen to music emanating from an open window on the fourth floor of a block of flats. Yep, the music has to be *1973*, by James Blunt. Absolutely great, the year I got married. I clap, delighted. Out of the window pops a head and a bloke, not young, gives the thumbs up at my appreciation.

Beverley: **Nature Notes from Lockdown**

On Monday I discover the council has instructed that the caravan sites and their access to the beaches near my home are to remain closed to prevent an influx of tourists. Although I live in the middle of the countryside, I cannot walk in the fields, as they are all full of young cattle, horses, and sheep with lambs. How frustrating is that? I am surrounded by fields, the low tide is laid out in front of my house and there is open sea all the way to the Isle of Man and America, but no way to get access to it! What will happen when the water is warm enough for swimming? I usually swim a mile every day as soon as the sea temperature reaches 14 degrees. What a disaster! I have to take my car to the estuary access point on the A75 and am nervous the police may stop me parking (following the incident last weekend in the Highlands), so I decide to conceal my car beside the little café, not to go there at weekends or when there is more than one other car.

As I slip and slide, armed with my trusty stick, through the rushes, tread cautiously across the slippery mud and ford the little burn, I catch sight of a bright patch of white, far out on the estuary mudflats. I get out my binoculars. Swans: about 30 of them. As I get closer, I can hear them chattering urgently with their beautiful, mournful, haunting voices: whooper swans. They are moving round and round in a tight group, sometimes lying down and silent, then all standing up and chatting. I watch them as I walk – a great debate going on. As I return, just as the light begins to fade, the swans all get up with a great cry, open their wings and rise as one, chattering all the time, flying low at first and then rising slowly, still trumpeting melodiously all the time, they fly off towards the north west. Have I just witnessed a flight plan being prepared and the beginning of their great annual flight to Iceland, which they will complete without stopping, ready for the breeding season? The next evening I return for my walk and to see if there is any sign of the swans, who have been around on the estuary for some weeks, but they have gone. With a clear still night, last night, I hope they have completed their long journey. Flying at 8,000 feet they should be there by now.

As I walk along the hard sand, I hear the unmistakable sound of ravens, and there they are. A pair, high up, tumbling over and over each other, rising up again and then falling in their extraordinary courtship display, while still flying forward at speed. What a beautiful feat of aerial acrobatics. My first two sneaky coastal walks well rewarded!

Ann G: **In Exile**

At first glance the sands look empty, denuded, abandoned. Down at the rippling water's edge are scatterings of clam shells which crunch underfoot. The gulls hop in the shallows. Further back are the rocks with their myriad pools. A father inches his children along the pipeline stretching out towards the sea. While the tide is out it's safe and far enough away from other people.

There are a few other people on Portobello beach. A younger couple with a dog materialise and swerve away to ensure a safe distance. They seem so ghostly, though, as if not wholly there. It feels like a waking dream, haunting each breath as we walk together. We're in a bubble in a strange and unfamiliar world.

We laugh at our clumsy, old-person efforts to clamber through the groynes and we talk, of course. Shared words can help so much in isolation. Increasingly that's where we live – in our heads – in our memories – in our conversations. It's words that keep us grounded and hold us safe in space and time. We talk of family the most. How hard it is for them. How well they're doing. The challenges they face. The grandchildren we miss. And New Galloway.

"I'm beginning to think we can't go. What do you think?"

"Give it a day or two. We don't have to decide till the last minute."

Then Londoners, decanting to second homes in Cornwall, are being roundly denounced and the game is up.

We read about the Glenkens on Facebook and in emails that circulate. New Galloway has been so central to our lives, but the immediacy of that involvement is fading. A lot seems to be going on without us that sounds heart-warming, but we can't help wondering where all these volunteers are coming from. Last time we looked we were nearly all in our seventies or eighties, hence now very firmly in lockdown. There's a new dynamic afoot in this brave new world.

"It's been so sudden. Last time we were there was less than a month ago."

"I know. It's funny, things didn't just stop dead, instantly. The lockdown crept up on us gradually, but at a really fast pace of creeping!"

Now we're exiled.

It sounds too dramatic, and the wind whips our words out over the water towards Fife, laughing at us, but the words do matter and we repeat them often. The variations and possibilities are endless. Three cruise ships sit anchored on the Firth, their lights beginning to twinkle in the distance. Their empty abandonment reminds us of our empty cottage and our thoughts turn once again to New Galloway.

When we get home from our daily walk, we settle down to do some more work on the latest grant bid for the Town Hall. We're hoping to employ a part-time project worker there when this is all over.

"The community in New Galloway is thriving," we write. We hope it's still true.

Cath: **Funerals**

Only a fortnight ago my husband Geoff performed his last duty as a lay reader for Kirkcudbright Parish Church.

He conducted the funeral of an old lady who was almost 109. A remarkable person who had lived independently until she was 104, then in a care home.

She had no immediate family as her only child had died aged 10. Her husband was a farmer; she had been a primary school teacher. The funeral was nearly a month after her death; her nieces and nephews treasured her and were coming from America and the south of England.

Then came travel bans, cancelled flights, and rules for conducting funerals.

In the end there were about eight to ten mostly local people, including the undertakers and gravediggers, standing well apart. No relatives. No refreshments. Not even a handshake. Then we went back home.

On the way back, I was struck by the sadness of it all - that the lady's passing and burial had been so unmarked, almost a pauper's funeral. No shared sorrow and social communication of memories and stories from all those years. No chance of a rare family gathering which such occasions usually generate. No reminiscences, appreciation and comfort given and received.

This is the way of it now. This old lady did not die of Covid-19, nor do the vast majority of those who die every day. Undertakers and celebrants deal with death daily. But now, instead of being able to offer their traditional comfort and support, they are constrained by the new rules. We know that families can hold a memorial gathering or celebration later on, but when? There will be thousands. Grief and sadness floating around with no focus or destination.

Many people nearing the end of their life take comfort in planning their own funeral, choosing hymns and music, a burial plot, the whole celebration. How sad to know that even if their family want to carry out their wishes, they are unable to do so. My parents died only seven months apart just over four years ago. I am grateful that we were able to arrange the very personal funeral services for both of them. I am glad they are no longer around to worry about now. They were remembered in a special way both communally and individually.

Maybe, when all this is over, we will spend the first few months filling our time attending the memorial services for those who are gone, but not forgotten.

Ros: **It's Spring and Nobody Will Stop It**

Io, my seven-year-old daughter: "Mummy, I don't really want to do Morale any more." Morale means brushing your hair, and your teeth, and making the bed. Morale means eating (vaguely) at meal times and going to bed (vaguely) at bedtime. I realise it's more important for me than it is for her. She is quite happy - delighted, in fact - to drift and dream, and not wash, and live on oatcakes and honey, and let imaginary games unfold over many days. I still have to work, and wash up, and bring wood in, and pay the council tax. Being a grown up feels like a bit of a raw deal.

And yet the child in me stirs and wakens. The sun shines, the kites wheel in the sky above, spring unfurls all around. I find renewed excitement in planting seeds, baking bread, riding my bike, finding violets (my most favourite flower ever) in their secret hiding places in the woods. Lines from an ee cummings poem keeps running through my head: 'run …/(…dance cry/sing for its Spring/… but nobody will stop it/With All The Policemen In The World'. It becomes the best thing ever to have a gutsy seven-year-old companion to hang out with.

At night, I appreciate the warmth of her mammal body snuggled up next to me in bed. She has taken to sleeping with me again after many years in her own room. I breathe her in, luxuriate in the warm dampness of her hair, the weight of her limbs thrown across mine. The words of an older fellow-villager who lives alone, met along the lane on an evening walk, haunt me whenever I think of them: "Might it be that I never touch another human being again?" My friend tells me that maybe we shouldn't be stroking our cats any more; some tigers in Seattle Zoo have become infected with Covid-19.

A birthday gift arrives from my sister: a book on wild foods and foraging. I soon find the section on violets. To my delight, I discover that violets are connected to the legend of Io. When Jupiter changed his beloved Io into a white heifer to protect her from the jealousy of his wife, Juno, he caused violets to grow as fitting food for her. Reading on, I get goosebumps; 'It is said that violets flowering in the autumn are a portent for a deadly epidemic'. I distinctly remember finding violets growing at the foot of the north gable of my house last November. In my wonder I even showed them to the postman.

For my daily 'one form of exercise' I take another wander through the woods, which I have re-named the Forest of Arden because of the many chance encounters I have had there over the past three weeks. (I always thought the plot line of *As You Like It* was wildly improbable, but now I find myself relishing being Rosalind and realising that absolutely anything can happen, and probably will.) On my way back I find, on a shady bank, a tangle of purest white violets. Does such a thing exist? Who knows? As some kind of proof of this dreamtime, I pluck one, and bring it home to press in the pages of Ram Dass's *Be Here Now*.

Christine: **We'll Stand Together**

I once wrote a poem about winning.

We all had a cause,
We worked as a team
And nothing we did was a trouble
For we knew very well that whatever we did
There were others out there doing double.

We may feel helpless but if we pool our resources we can make a difference. A village is a small community and in that lies its strength. Everyone knows everyone else, and a crisis brings everyone together. People walk dogs, deliver shopping and papers, collect prescriptions, and become an army of volunteers willing to spend time phoning and keeping in touch with people who are lonely and isolated, and we all feel that sometimes.

A village is not just a collection of people. It is a living entity.

April 6th to April 13th

Police move on
Easter sunbathers...

Queen's broadcast:
"coronavirus will not overcome us"...

UK records Europe's
worst daily toll = 980 deaths...

PM leaves
hospital...

Beverley: Holy Week

Holy Week. The churches are all closed and congregations prohibited. Our Rector will be celebrating the usual services for Holy Week in each of his charges, St. Mary's in Gatehouse and Greyfriars in Kircudbright, but by himself. I have been asked to change the altar frontal in St. Mary's from green to white on Thursday morning early, before the Maundy Thursday service at 11 am when he will celebrate the Last Supper. This is my usual job as I helped to make the frontals many years ago. The Rector will then strip the altar in preparation for Good Friday's service and will put back the white frontal before he celebrates Easter at 9.30 am on Sunday – all alone. The Rector sends his congregations the Bible readings and prayers for the week, so we can celebrate with him, in our own homes.

Good Friday dawns; a sparkling, sunny day. We would normally have held an ecumenical Walk of Witness in Gatehouse, carrying one of

the three crosses which have been planted outside St. Mary's. I decide to do my Walk of Witness or Stations of the Cross up to the top of the hill where I placed a memorial stone to my beloved husband after his death five years ago. The stone is a huge granite boulder, just the perfect height for sitting on, or for children to climb on and jump off. This hill, while not very high, punches above its weight, like Cat Bells in Cumbria. It has a magnificent view of Cairnsmore of Fleet, Galloway Forest Park and most of our farm. It was my husband's daily morning walk and a favourite with his parents, where they used to play 'flying' games with the children in the strong breezes that nearly always blow there. The way up is quite rough and steep and takes me about three quarters of an hour to get there and half an hour back. Armed with a warm coat, my trusty stick and a knapsack containing my Bible, reading references, prayers and a bottle of water, I start my journey of reflection. The blackie sheep have been brought down from the higher hills and there is one ewe with two newly born lambs. I always think of them as 'proper sheep' as opposed to the Border Leicester/Texel crosses I used to lamb in the shed.

There is very little wind when I get to the top. It is warm and the air is full of the song of larks. As I sit down on the stone, a snipe rises from a damp patch of reeds. I slowly read the prayers, lessons, psalm and Gospel for Good Friday out loud so I can share it with my husband and the larks. A day to contemplate life, sadness and loss, death and sacrifice, but with the foreknowledge of the promise of Easter, so appropriate for this difficult time of pestilence, when all over the world so many are ill and dying; frightened, suffering, grieving and alone. Whether we are religious or not, whatever we believe, we must all keep faith with the certainty that 'this too will pass' and the determination that we will come out of this terrible time, stronger and kinder and with a greater appreciation of the wonderful world we live in. How fragile is this precious planet? Can we learn to be happy with less, to care for our families, loved ones and those less fortunate than ourselves and remember all the good things which emerged during lockdown?

To keep hold of them and not to go back to our old, greedy, uncaring ways.

Mike: The Subjunctive World

My daughter arrives tomorrow. My grandsons will jump out of the car desperate to start the chocolate egg hunt. It's been a highlight of their Easter for as long as they can remember.

But they won't be staying long. We set out next week on our 'Big Spring Trip': to Shrewsbury, Bristol, Bath and beyond, an odyssey of reconnections and reminiscence around old friends.

Well, that's what it says on the kitchen calendar, although scarcely legibly, what with the palimpsest of scorings out and sad deletions.

And so we live our parallel lives. "Today we would have been…," we muse, looking at the cancelled world on our wall. "Tonight we would have been going to Caroline's lecture…," we say, thinking of her anxious weeks of preparation. "Tomorrow we would have been travelling to

Megan's," we continue. She's back in England after 40 years in Helsinki but her son, she tells us, returned to his native Finland. "Where they invented self-isolation," she adds with Nordic drollery.

Life in this subjunctive world is hectic. Through the proscenium of our calendar we watch extremely busy versions of ourselves tear round the country, juggling multiple bookings. Comfortable in the dress circle of our new world, we watch bemused at such frantic on-stage folly. We can feel quite tired just thinking of what we should have been doing 'today'.

How often have we said, "Imagine an empty day - with all that time to ourselves"?

Just imagine.

Well, here it is.

Mary: **Weight and Lightness**

I feel my life is divided between weight and lightness.

The lightness of having an empty diary, no commitments, no musts, shoulds or have-to-dos. A walk in the countryside, work in the garden, time to read. Knowing my son, my sister and other family members are fine. Phone calls with friends. The occasional bubble of pure joy that wells up for no apparent reason. A sense that some of the lightness will continue after this is over.

The weight of guilt at daring to feel happy when people are getting sick, dying, often dying alone without family. Of not being one of the thousands of volunteers helping others. Anger at how this pandemic has been mismanaged. Fury when I learn the masks and gloves and aprons in warehouses were stockpiled for a post-Brexit emergency, at how care homes are being pushed to the bottom of the pile. One woman is in tears. She has been sent 300 single-use face masks – her staff have 700 visits to make in a week.

The weight and the lightness.

This spring, the daffodils have been amazing. The last time we had such glorious shows of daffodils was the year of Foot and Mouth. Is that true or is it because in the midst of a crisis we open our eyes wider; are more observant, or susceptible to beauty?

The death statistics are increasing but still, when I hear the numbers, I feel they are given without any context. Don't we need a baseline? How many people die every day anyway? It doesn't make sense to me. I found an article on *The Journal of Medical Ethics* blog which attempts to provide some context. I hate feeling so ignorant and take no comfort in the fact that even medical and scientific experts are too.

I still enjoy looking at my appointment-free diary – except when I notice my hair appointment won't happen.

Carol: **Covid Defiance**

I cut my hair today
And dyed it red in oft-remembered adolescent rage
At how the politicians of the world
Have cracked the whip and left the poor
The disenfranchised, the immigrants
The nurses and the doctors
To sacrifice their families
Their lives
Whilst they live on in cushioned isolation
Rewarded for their solitude
Unlike the elderly
Left to uncertain fate in Homes
Now ill-equipped to Care

I cut my hair today
And basked in compliments from WhatsApp friends
Then felt the guilt of too much joy
Am I fiddling while my country burns?
Should I keep on laughing?
Refuse to be drawn by the Daily Doom-and-Gloom
Of news and social media, of friends struck down
Of fear for family too far away?

I cut my hair today
And dyed it red in defiance
My own "Sod You!" to this rampaging ill
Perhaps tomorrow I shall dye it green

Roger: **Snapshots**

My action man is Alphie, the Jack Russell, who is set on confronting our local urban Mr Fox. At dusk we approach the woodland quietly, and the reward? A grey shape loping along, tail floating behind him. Alphie is in doggie heaven but not me, restraining him. Mr Foxy disappears, rapido, beneath the fence. We try again at midnight. Out we go, only to catch sight of Mr Brown Foxy, in and out, and over the walls of people's gardens, then parading down the street. He doesn't know he has made the day for my Jack Russell.

At midday, seated on the black seat, which is boasting yet more flowers, I was presented with a magic parade, advancing toward me: three family parties of two adults with young daughters walking between them. Each daughter had on a vast, coloured, top hat, bit unsteady, but so magical; a sight to watch exiting down the hill slowly, slowly, wobbling.

The community always turns out in force for the NHS celebration of thanks each week with clapping. Whenever I witness this, I remember how in Bangladesh I was once asked, "Is it true, Mr Roger, that in England, if sick, I could ask a hospital for help and they would not ask for money first?"

Leonie: **Wildlife Garden Journal**

Without fanfare, the leaves on trees and shrubs uncurl. New wildflowers appear in succession; dandelions with sun faces have replaced coltsfoot, forget-me-not buds are bursting blue. The air fills with the drone of queen bumblebees, tree bumbles as well as buff-tailed and red-tailed. Peacocks and small tortoiseshells flutter by in the sun.

The dominant garden character is the male blackbird that nests in the cypress tree. I have been watching him throughout the day for the past fortnight. Now that the nest is finished the hen is mainly sitting, coming out only to grab a worm or two. His daily routine becomes apparent. He keeps guard from the boundary fences, south then west in turn, sits immobile looking out in the early light, a dark shape with drooping wings.

Constant in his devotions he drops low from the lookout and makes for the water bath. There follows a flurry of feathers, an enthusiastic broadcasting of water-drops like broken strings of pearls. A nearby cotoneaster is perfect for drying off and preening in the sun. He checks the east boundary, landing on the fence with a dip of the head and a cocked tail that makes him look impressive. Under the protection of the spiny berberis he takes a small breakfast, tossing over piles of birch leaves with abandon in search of tasty morsels.

It's time to check on the nest. He disappears into the green depth, emerging later from a secret exit, crosses open ground in a headlong rush, gold dagger of his bill ready to take on all-comers: a male from the neighbouring garden and then a female who has dared to use his bath. Then he's off again, this time to chase a sparrow who has alighted too close to the nest. He will have to keep this up for a while yet. Later, on his rounds, he takes a second bath.

Gordon: **Chaos and Confusion**

As the leg improves, I'm able to help around the house a bit more, not that there's much to do. News worse about the virus. No one seems to know what to do, partly because testing is so sparse we don't really know how widespread the virus is, and if you don't know your facts you can't put together a proper response, or even, in the case of Trump, a coherent response. Who believes authority anymore?

But I can continue with writing at speed now. First book has gone out to friends to read and comment, finished draft of a second novel called *Delicious*, about a fit tough girl who gets a thrill out of subduing men. Don't worry, nothing crude. Now looking for anyone who wants to read it and comment on it. Looking at agents and other stuff on getting both books published so still keeping very busy. Third book on the go, which features a natural disaster like a pandemic, but this is a severe magnetic storm. Fourth book being built within the Glenkens Writers Group. What you can do with lockdown and a broken leg!

I have written fiction about the misbehaviour and corruption of those in authority. Now it's happening in real life. What do they think, standing up in the Downing Street briefings with serious faces telling us what to do, but forgetting that the rules apply to them as well! Then the people at the top get sick and/or get caught out breaking the rules. And the stupidity! That Raab saying he's sure that Boris will pull through! Only his medical team can say that.

On the other hand, there's so much goodwill amongst ordinary people, locally and nationally willing to volunteer to do anything they can turn their hands to. What did they say about army leadership in WW1? 'Lions led by donkeys'. Perhaps that applies now? And I say that as a Tory party member.

Plaster cast off yesterday afternoon and, "Yippee!!!", bones have unexpectedly set perfectly and no further treatment needed; just keep to tarmac for runs for the next three months to avoid falls while I build up again. I can get outside, but only into the restricted world we now live in with the economy crashed. A friend who gives driving lessons and runs a hostel in the Highlands has been ruined. Always busy, suddenly she's completely without work and income except for looking at government support schemes. Should we have followed the Swedes and kept things open? Getting the economy up and running again will be a massive job and much capacity will be gone.

But isn't it quiet? Can we transform into a poorer economy in money terms, but a richer one in terms of the quality of life? It'll help with global warming too.

Christine: Confounded Confusion

I'm very confused and emotional this week.

I thought I was OK until I read the newspaper. I didn't know the difference between lockdown and social isolation. I thought that you go into lockdown if you have the virus, but social isolation means you can still go out if you stand two metres away from another person. The information does not seem to be very clear on this point.

I can't imagine how I can stay alone for a long period; I am talking to myself as it is, and if anyone asks me how I am managing, it is very hard to hold in my feelings. It's past 6.30 pm and at 7 I shall be able to take Jack out for a poo, and then perhaps come back, have a glass of something nice and watch something rubbishy on the telly.

Ros: **Belonging**

I don't get a walk until the evening, by which time the sun has gone behind the hill to the west and my usual Forest of Arden walk will be all in shadow. With a pang I remember the Craigs: the sunlit hills to the north-east of the village that I used to scramble up almost daily as a child. Since I moved back to the village, they've been off-limits: despite the right to roam, the landowner has run barbed wire along all the villagers' back garden gates, which for the past hundred years or more had opened into 'his' field.

It's not that I'm fearful; more that my walks take me into a soft, meditative frame of mind, in which any manner of confrontation would feel brutally intrusive. Tonight, I feel defiant. I have walked there all my life! I was here long before he was! It's a glorious April evening, the sheep have had their lambs, I know exactly how to walk with care and respect across farmland and I don't have a dog with me!

I set off, and quickly realise that it's no longer possible to hop, as I used to as a child, over the fence behind the Crockett memorial; it now has barbed wire running along it too. I strike up several-metres-apart conversation with the visitors in the end house, up from England for the Covid duration.

"Oh, we've been going up there nearly every day," they say, and point me to the new way round, past the two new bungalows.

As I strike out across the fields and start to ascend the hill, my heart sings. I know every step of this path like I know my own body. By the time I mount the summit, tears are streaming down my cheeks. Why do I wait so meekly for the permission or invitation of others? Why do I assume myself unwelcome, an unwanted intruder? What will it take for me to understand that I have a right to feel I belong? Here, perhaps, more than anywhere. Will I spend my whole life pulling away from the people and places that are important to me, testing these relationships to breaking point in my fear of being either rejected or colonised? I scramble through the still-brown bracken, the heather, the tussocks in the boggy bits. I stoop down here and there to watch a bumble bee; to get a rich, velvety eyeful of my beloved wild violets; to pick up a shiny hazel wand; to run my fingers through the silky grass.

Three rowans grow close to the summit. Like three wise women they stand, their roots holding them firmly in the ground as the capricious April wind catches their newly-budding leaves. Beyond them I can see right across to the Rhinns of Kells and the Carsphairn hills. The loch gleams northwards in a sleek curve, speedwell-blue. A generous bevy of red kites - another more recent addition to this landscape than I am - silently surf the wind channels overhead.

I feel this place catch at the hem of my skirt, and tug. No bluster: just a quiet revealing of all that is most beautiful and familiar and true to me.

On the way back down the hill I stop at the S.R.Crockett memorial and read Robert Louis Stevenson's tribute.

Blows the wind today, and the sun and the rain are flying,
Blows the wind on the moors today and now,
Where about the graves of the martyrs the whaups are crying,
My heart remembers how!

April 13th to April 20th

Furlough for nine million
to cost £30 billion...

NHS workers claim
still short of PPE...

Higher death rate
in BAME communities...

Lockdown
extended three weeks...

Trump withdraws US
from WHO...

Ann G: **At Sea**

I'm feeling more at sea this week. I think I've come unanchored, my mind adrift and washed ashore in unexpected places. Time has come unhinged. I wake in childhood with my parents' voices, or in a flurry of anxiety about my babies – all now grown with families of their own, of course.

Reality is a different, unfamiliar place now. Our points of focus, our commitments, held us in their thrall and often kept us far too busy, but hold us there they did. We knew that world so well. We knew our role in it. Both time and place now seem unknowable and I float, untethered and vaguely alarmed about where my thoughts are taking me.

Feeling at sea is more than a metaphor for me because I'm here in Portobello, right by the sea. We walk there every day, enveloped in the immediacy of the waves and wind. There is familiarity, but there's so much missing. We should be in New Galloway by rights. That's where we feel at home. It's where our thoughts keep turning.

Pack up the car, drive down, loving the scenery as we go, unpack and decant ourselves once more into the cottage. See our friends, schedule our meetings, visit family, adore our little grandson, relax into the village; marvel again at how every visit to the community shop involves bumping into so many people we know.

That oh-so-central part of our routine has gone. There's a free-floating emptiness around. Our world is different without that focus.

I guess I just feel a bit lost – and sad. I saw on Facebook the plea from Glenkens Medical Practice for part-time second-homers not to visit and I felt so hurt. Absurd, I know, as I totally support the message and we will, indeed, not come down while this lasts. It just underlined the sense of exile. We really are outsiders now.

And yet, my floating mind can still drop anchor when needs be. This afternoon I had to answer questions on the latest funding bid to Blackcraig Wind Farm during a pre-planned phone call with Foundation Scotland to talk it through. For half an hour I was transported back into that familiar reality where I knew my way around.

Then out into the cold northeasterly, blowing off the sea.

Beverley: Shape to Life

With lockdown I have lost the normal shape to my life – the routine which gives it backbone. Life has become a steep, upskilling slope – Zoom, YouTube, Livestreaming and trying to keep all the 'techy' bits of equipment in one's life from hitting the buffers with no access to an IT expert anymore.

So, what I need is a new routine.

6 am: I continue to get up early, a relic from my days as a shepherdess during and after Foot and Mouth disease in 2001. I decide two sets of clothes are all I need, one on and one lot in the wash! That way

I don't have to do any ironing – just take them out of the tumble dryer and fold them up. My standards have definitely slipped.

7 am: An hour of Tai Chi, yoga and meditation with church readings for the day.

8 am: Breakfast and the news (if I can bear it – it is so boring and repetitive these days).

9 am: Washing up, cleaning kitchen and bathroom, occasional vacuuming and not much dusting.

I have a regular Zoom yoga twice a week, two Zoom coffee parties and a monthly Zoom book club - wonderfully disciplined, as our host mutes us all and lets us out one by one. No talking over each other anymore!

I plan to do some writing every day and work in the garden which, being only two years old, is still very much a work in progress. I order plants online which take ages to come. I'm lucky enough still to have my gardener for a couple of hours a week to mow the lawn, trim the hedges and help me with the planting.

I go for a walk every day. As I am so slow these days I allow myself two hours, the equivalent of a fit person's one hour of allowed daily exercise! I still walk on the low tide line surreptitiously and on the tracks at my old home.

6 pm: I make my supper and eat it watching the news – I so miss having anyone to talk to at mealtimes or discuss the news with. Before Covid-19, and since being on my own, I have entertained friends and family to lunch and dinner at least four times a week.

6.30 pm: I find my way into the Metropolitan Opera website on my rarely-used tablet and watch their livestreaming free opera of the day. After 7 pm I no longer answer the telephone and retreat into my evenings in fantasyland: sometimes opera and ballet, sometimes National Theatre productions. I have been trying to work out how much I will owe them as a donation for helping me to survive. Strangely, concerts with no human voices just make me cry.

Carol: **A Visit from the Black Dog**

It creeps, it creeps
Along the garden paths
Or up the stairs
There is no boundary
To shield me from its dark approach
It creeps
Until it locks its jaws
About my feet, and I become
Immobilised
I'd thought myself beyond its reach
Felt safe, and calm
So why this visitation?
This looming presence of the Big Black Dog?

It creeps, I weep
Along my garden paths
And up my stairs
No solace in the song of birds today
The Black Dog always at my back
Glowering
Willing me to shed more tears
Is this the rage I cannot speak
Turned inwards,
Coaxing the Black Dog
From deep within my soul?
Can I tame it once again
And turn it back?

I need to scream

Margaret: **Marooned**

Benn Gunn in *Treasure Island* is marooned by Captain Flint and his self-serving, greedy, old boys' gang. They run the prototype of all hedge fund gaming, which in *Treasure Island* is called piracy. By the time the *Hispaniola* turned up, Ben Gunn was a crazy dreadlocked old man who hadn't spoken to another human being in 30 years. Ben Gunn is not the hero of *Treasure Island*. He is entirely incidental...

My marooning was in the Monachs, low-lying sandy islands off the North Uist coast. Those were the days when I sailed, not with pirates, but with bird ringers, from Sule Skerry to St Kilda. Bob, our skipper, knew my heart's desire was to land on uninhabited islands and remain there for as long as possible. To be alone on an island, by choice, is perfect, unassailable solitude. Being marooned is different.

I came ashore on Ceann Ear. Ringed plover scuttered over the tideline. Blue butterflies fluttered among the dunes. Sheep cropped the turf where bees drowsed over thrift and eyebright. I didn't stop. Siolaigh, the westernmost Monach, has a tall brick lighthouse; I never missed a lighthouse if I could help it. I had three strands to cross. The tide was just coming in. Shibhinis was surrounded by miles of gleaming sand. In those days I could run. The strand between Shibhinis and Ceann Iar is a two-minute crossing. Almost a mile to cross Ceann Iar, and here was the lighthouse across the sound where the sea was pouring through.

Pouring through... a glance at my watch. Oh my god. Panting back the length of Ceann Iar. The little crossing to Shibhinis. The sea a bit too near. Across Shibhinis as fast as I could. Ceann Ear in front of me. Sea, green over sand, streaming through the gap, rising as I looked. Marooned.

I had the walkie-talkie. "I thought you were supposed to know what you're doing? OK, the others have gone for a dive. Angus can pick you up when they get back. Couple of hours, maybe."

Shibhinis is a third of a mile by a quarter, its highest point 16 metres. Oystercatchers love it, but they are not marooned. I had some oatcakes in my pocket, as I always do at sea. I sat nibbling them. I'd known the tide was rising, but I'd somehow believed that time and tide would wait for me. Wherever did I learn such a big lie? Now I couldn't get off, Shibhinis looked bleak, almost hostile. A cold breeze crept across my back. Angus would come soon. Surely. I discovered I was really quite keen to get off.

Now I'm living on a different sort of island. I always wanted more solitude, but I had conditions. I wanted to be in charge of my island, and to leave when I'd had enough. My friends and family are marooned too. The whole world is marooned. I read in the newspaper that no one knows when the tide will go out again, or if a rescue ship will arrive. Choosing to be on an island is one thing. Being marooned is different.

Christine: **Friends and Neighbours**

My routine hasn't changed. I need something to keep me stable in the present situation. However I notice that I appreciate the company of the people I meet. It's a fellow-feeling. We are all in this together. I go up the road for a walk with my dog, and really look at the things I see. I realise how much I had missed. It's amazing to be able to talk to others not about the present situation, that goes beyond any speech, but as friends. I had a most interesting conversation with a man who was walking down the road. We had both watched a quiz on the TV the previous night and I chatted to him about it. Meanwhile, along comes someone else, whose dog uses shocking language at my Jack, who gives it back. Things are normal at times! I am certainly not going to be as shy and uncommunicative as I once was, and will be all the better for it.

Rose: **Easter**

Most days there's some contact, a phone call or connecting on screen like inter-galactic travellers. Comparing notes with friends on our lockdown lives, we're still not clear about how to behave and have different understandings of the new vocabulary. We have lived mostly as challengers of the established order, disinclined to jump to Boris and Dominic's tune.

Our family decides to create a virtual household between houses. We have to check each other out, respect each others' anxieties as we go along. It doesn't feel right to move about at will. I struggle to stop being part of my grandchildren's daily lives. We find ways to connect discreetly through short trips to back gardens.

We draw our wagons in a circle and apply the rules to those outside the stockade, turning friends away if they approach. My treasured neighbour comes across to see how we are. We have an awkward conversation about what's OK and she runs out of the garden in tears. We contact a valued friend and tell her not to come into our house or garden. Our co-grandparents are coming to the village. Will they call in for socially-distanced coffee in our sunny garden? We phone back and ask them not to come.

I set out early on Sunday morning, an Easter bunny in pyjamas, delivering egg boxes full of painted stones. There's a note on the car outside the other family house. When I get home I notice that we have one too. It's a copy of the letter from 10 Downing Street, damp from the night air, with yellow highlighter running down next to the words: 'you *must* stay at home'. I'm stopped in my tracks. Ours are the only cars to be marked out in this way. The village no longer feels benign. Someone has been observing our behaviour. Are they reminding or warning us? But they are right. We have made our own interpretation of the rules. It's not OK. I feel bruised and exposed. I'm embarrassed to own up to bending the rules.

I've upset the neighbours, known or unknown. That evening we are on our own, marking the fourth anniversary of our move to the village. We share a photo of our celebration table on the family WhatsApp group.

Cathy: **Covert Covid Thought**

Do the Sprite thing
Stay Gnome
Protect the National Elf Service
By Elf isolation…

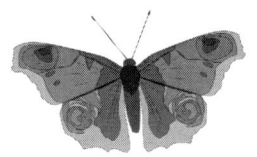

Ros: **The Deciding Tree**

Just as I'm placing two freshly-baked loaves on the gatepost for my friend, who has cycled ten miles in sun and wind to collect them, the Fleet Fish van passes and comes to stop a few yards along the road. "Are you selling?" I call.

"Well, we've gone entirely online now, and you need to pre-order, but I do have some scallops here."

Scallops! If I was on Death Row, I'd totally choose scallops for my last supper. "I'll take a dozen," I say impulsively. My purse feels unfamiliar in my hand, the £20 note like Monopoly money. When was the last time I opened my handbag?

Afterwards, it occurs to me that there's something kind of biblical about the loaves and the fish sharing their moment in the sun. 'For heaven's sake,' Io has taken to adding to many of her sentences. I wonder where she picked that up. Do they say it in the Tintin books? There's something sweet and old-fashioned and urgent about it. It makes things imperative: "Mummy, can you make up your mind, for heaven's sake?"

It's been feeling as though the Covid crisis has taken the People and the Practicalities out of the equation and brought me face to face, unadulteratedly, with Place. All set to leave, I was: the day before the Covid curtain fell, I had visited three primary schools in the south side of Glasgow and found the one that felt just right for Io. I'd been to a couple of estate agents and had it confirmed that yes, I'd be in a position to buy the right kind of flat in the right area. Work lined up, house on the market. It was all in the palm of my hand, on the tip of my tongue. It was a bit daunting, making a big move like this on my own as a single mum, but I was ready: excited about city life, work opportunities, cultural diversity, using my brain, going out to eat. A new chapter.

Climbing the vast Wellingtonia by the pond, a memory surfaces, and I glance across at Io, wondering whether she is old enough for me to share it with her. "Did you know that when I was married to the daddy of your two big sisters, I was sitting on this very branch when I decided I did not want to stay married to him any more?"

She fixes me with her beady eyes: "So, this is the Deciding Tree," she says. Then, climbing over onto another branch: "This is the Thinking Branch, and when you've done your Thinking, you move over to that one to Decide."

I'm the person who can't bear to thin seedlings: I feel like a murderess. I want them all to grow. But sometimes you have to choose.

Gordon: **More Chaos in High Places**

Lots to worry about nationally, but not personally, as I'm getting out now. The leg is improving. There are opportunities to chat to people in their gardens on my daily walk in this lovely weather. Some are finding the lockdown tedious, but we've got a small garden and a pile of stuff to do. I've started to read a couple of books in the pile and now find them uninteresting.

I worry about damage to the economy. So many businesses will disappear that our choice of books, clothes, hardware, domestic goods etc. will become mostly online with big monopolies like Amazon gobbling up the market. The government will have to raise a lot of taxation when it's all over, or let inflation rip, or both. Pensions for people like us will be hit, with the triple lock out of the window. There will have to be new taxes, possibly even something communistic like a savings tax. But all governments are worried about high earners and multimillionaires running for cover to tax havens so it'll be a light touch for them as usual. The block on bank dividends will hit many ordinary savers who rely on them for regular income, unlike the rich. It bodes ill for them when this is all over and many other dividends will no longer be paid. In some countries there's going to be unrest, even revolution. The 'Establishment' will try to get us back to business as usual but it's difficult to see how that could work now.

Hopefully, Heathrow Runway 3 and HS2 are no longer affordable - they were never really needed anyway. As a train enthusiast I would love to see the money spent on improving existing services and re-opening closed lines like the Port Line from Dumfries to Stranraer, preferably after getting rid of huge amounts of regulation and the dead hand of the rail management people.

Seeds have arrived, so a short zzzzz and then into the garden sunshine, maybe even chatting with neighbours.

Mary: At Home and Abroad

In recent years I've worked as a seasonal museum attendant in the summer months. The museums are closed now and no one knows when they will re-open. Someone from the council's Human Resources Department phones to ask if I'd be willing, after training, to work in customer services.

Being a freelance, I'm conditioned to saying yes to any offer of work and I agree to the manager calling me for further discussion. Even as I put the phone down I feel stress levels rising. I absolutely hate the idea of leaving seclusion.

The DH has asthma and is a medium-to-high risk. He is, understandably, much more worried than I about the virus. He even shouted at a customer in the supermarket for coming too close. He was unhappy at the thought of me mixing with other people and potentially bringing the virus home. I was relieved to have an excuse, even though saying my husband wasn't happy about me going out to work made me feel like a 1950s housewife. I pointed out I've been obeying the rules about staying at home and didn't feel it was right the council should ask me to break them. The man from HR agreed – apparently others have said the same. I was so relieved I did a little happy dance at my desk.

What is happening in the rest of the world while we are fed a non-stop diet of coronavirus news? It's very difficult to find out anything not Covid-19 related. Saudi Arabia and its coalition partners (which include us) declared a ceasefire to stop bombing Yemen – the first case of Covid-19 is reported next day. The ceasefire didn't last. Syria, Libya, refugee camps – every humanitarian crisis suddenly has an extra layer of misery and pain added.

I spot my neighbour across the road at his upstairs window. He is over 70, a cancer survivor, and lives alone. Time passes slowly for him. He counts the cars, making bets with himself about how many white ones he'll see before a red one comes along. I check if he needs anything. He's been overwhelmed by gifts of food from people who care.

Mike: Clapped Out

So we've clapped for the NHS.

That felt good. Applause echoing up and down the village. Heartfelt of course. Well-reported nationwide by media desperately seeking some cheer in a bleak world. Just a hint of national complacency perhaps - did some commentator say, 'Blitz Spirit'? I hope not.

So another Friday and our health service 'heroes' can wake safe in the knowledge that they are appreciated.

And they had better cling on to that, because clapping will bring damn all else.

It won't bring them enough colleagues to share the work.

It won't bring them enough protective gear.

It won't bring the poorest paid anything like a living wage.

And it won't undo the four wasted years since the 2016 pandemic exercise revealed there was not enough kit.

So we had better keep clapping, and a bit more besides perhaps?

Will we be at our politicians' doors - when not conveniently corralled off the streets - demanding the NHS is properly funded, staffed and equipped - for the next time?

Will we be on the streets - no, not doorsteps - streets, when our leader, he whose life was saved, with such delicious irony, by immigrant nurses, tells us that economic recovery requires austerity? And while we will all be in it together of course, it would be economically unwise to tax his friends.

And how will we express ourselves when the details leak out - because do not expect any transparency - of the UK-US trade deal? Coronavirus may well have paralysed both economies but the corporate lobbyists of Washington are alive and well, still pressing for a profitable foothold in the NHS.

Our admiration and gratitude are sincere as we stand at our doors, clapping, with the evening breeze off the east, and the sun setting behind Black Craig of Dee. Our clapping is worthwhile, but not sufficient. And if we are not prepared to do much more than clap - it will have been in vain.

April 20th to April 27th

Scottish Covid
patient numbers falling...

Protests against
second home owners...

Devastating moorland fire
near Mossdale...

Social distancing
for rest of year forecast...

Carol: **What I Have Become**

I am become a child

Jumping at shadows

Never sure who, or what, to trust

Escaping into the fantasy

Of cartoons, comics, and colouring-in

I do not watch the news

The scary adult world

Is too grown-up for me

So I pretend it isn't there

I am become a child

Needing a hug, a cuddle on a lap

A sticking-plaster on the knee
Of my grazed emotions
But where to turn?
There's so much love, so much care
And yet –
Such a needy child

I know she's always been there
This small, fragile being
But I have kept her deep within
And played the raucous adolescent
These many, many years
So now she shouts for recognition
And thus, I am become a child

Beverley: **Drama and New Beginnings**

This has been a week of drama and new beginnings. The huge fire near Mossdale raged for four days, filling the whole of the Fleet estuary with smoke and lighting up the sky at night for miles around. We could see it creeping nearer and nearer to the Fleet valley and feared for our farms and those of neighbours on the east side of the valley. What a mercy the wind changed direction through 90 degrees and blew the fire back over the burnt-out land where it finally went out.

This was the week I started making scrubs for the NHS. I had hoped to work for the food bank but was deemed too old in the end. I was delighted to find something useful to do at last, having served on the WRVS emergency team for years, even if piecing the patterns together was rather a challenge.

On Wednesday I was due to have my hair cut. I had decided, having had long hair which I could put up for most of my life, that I would just let it grow. When the time came, however, I had a rush of blood to the head, washed my hair, seized the scissors, and with the help of my tri-folding mirror, gave it my all. To my amazement, the result was really rather good. I wonder if I dare do it again next month? But perhaps hairdressers will be open by then.

The weather is still amazing, so I take my courage in both hands and plunge into the loch for a swim! The water is only 12 degrees but wonderful and I manage to stay in for half an hour. Summer really is on its way! I normally swim in the sea every day from mid-April to the end of October, but the beaches here are still closed. I desperately hope they open by mid-May or I will feel very deprived.

Ros: **Sundowners Part 1**

Having enjoyed more sundown white wine spritzers and gin and tonics than usual since lockdown began, I decide in my holiday spirit slash boredom and despair to pack a G&T when Io and I go on our Sunday afternoon bike ride. Thus begins my foray into daytime drinking. Now, wide awake at 3 am for my first sleepless night in weeks, I vow to end it where it began. Who could have foretold the consequences of me lowering my guard, loosening up, letting my hair down?

It began benignly enough. We didn't cycle far, perhaps a mile out of the village. We found a sunlit, fallow field with open views to the south, which welcomed us in through a gate that was not just wide open but had been removed clean from its hinges. We found shelter from the wind in the lee of a rocky outcrop, where we happily set up home, made daisy chains, rolled down the hill, practised tying shoelaces and read our books. I opened the bottle of ready-mixed G&T and sipped it while Io ate some oatcakes. With every sip, the world obediently became simpler, lighter, full up to the brim of exactly where we were and what we were doing.

After a couple of hours of frolicking in the field, Io and I cycled home. By now, I could feel myself operating from the seam of irresponsibility that - to my shame, or pride, depending on which way the wind is blowing - runs immutably through me. We were having lots of fun though. We had a raucous game of dodgeball on the trampoline and ate rocket ice lollies for lunch.

Later we head over to our friend's house to drop off a loaf of bread I've baked for her. She lives alone, and has 'underlying health issues' (another new but already ubiquitous term) that mean she must 'self isolate' (and another) completely. She's in obvious distress. She tells us she's been watching all day as an orphan lamb in the field next to her house has been repeatedly rejected by its adoptive mother. It's beyond crying now, silently shivering, dying. In the end she could bear it no longer. Shortly before our arrival, she'd gone into the field and scooped it up, and was feeding it tiny amounts of warm water from a bottle.

So this is where it gets hazy, and a bit crazy. Somehow, in this strange situation, I find myself agreeing to take this pitiful, nearly-dead creature home with me. Is it Io's beseeching eyes, or my friend's palpable distress? Is it my own maternal or dyed-in-the-wool rescuer instinct? Is it the bloody G&T? But that was hours ago.

The lamb looks like it's going to die at any moment. I explain carefully to Io that this is the most probable outcome; and that if we take the lamb, it will most likely be a matter of caring for it as best we can in the short time it has left.

We bring the lamb into the kitchen to warm him by the Rayburn. His eyes are dull and he seems wholly unresponsive to the drops of warm water I dab onto his dry mouth. Then, suddenly - shockingly - he launches himself halfway to his feet and gulps down a dozen eggcups-full of water. It seems impossible that something so tiny and lifeless can summon up such a tidal wave of energy. I feel my heart lurch as I witness the force and ferocity of life's unfathomable fight for itself. The lamb wags his tail, bleats loudly and totters around the kitchen.

Io, who by now has named him Crispy, asks, "If he survives, can we keep him forever?" Oh dear...

Gordon: Too Many Lawyers and Accountants

As we are in a low population area, people can get about outside and go for walks, runs or cycle rides without tripping over each other and breaking the rules. We still seem able to get along with each other with few exceptions. But the law-makers are producing more and more new legislation which gets in the way of innovative people and businesses doing interesting things. Their influence at the top is permeating society, acting as a brake on change, wanting us back to the old 'normal'; a normal that elects people like Donald Trump, who don't believe in science or the laws of nature. The other side put Hilary Clinton up against him, so what did they expect? The Roman Empire collapsed because of weak leaders and out-of-control bureaucracy. Will we do the same, or will this virus give us the chance to rethink things?

The laws of nature are different from man-made laws. They can be understood or misunderstood but they can't be broken. For instance, to declare that Covid-19 is fake news doesn't cause it to vanish, it just means that many more lives will be lost. Denying global warming, building more roads, flying more is the route to oblivion. There has to be more innovation, more taking climate change seriously. We change or we are all DOOMED!

Can democracy save us or will it doom us? There are some good people elected but not enough. How do we elect good, competent people at all levels? Look at the process. You need to be selected by a political party. Then you have to get elected. If you do, you're just one voice amongst many and are part of the party machine so have to do as you're told. Very few independents get elected. Once elected, you can try to get a ministerial post, say transport. If you did, even if you get a bit of room to try new ideas, like no new roads and more rail, you'd have to be clever enough to make a dent in the civil service resistance to change. Inertia is a disease that could kill us all.

My recovery continues, mobility increasing, walking well but not yet running through our lovely countryside. Once I'm running again I won't feel the need to rant!

Mary: **Sad and Lazy**

I am becoming lazy. Attempts to tidy my study have been abandoned. It's a horrible mess with books, folders, papers strewn around the floor, photo albums piled on the chair and old diaries spilling out of boxes. Everything has ground to a halt. The weather is too nice to be stuck inside. In the garden I sit and read. I watch butterflies and bumblebees, listen to the birds. I occasionally do a bit of gardening but mostly I sit in the sunshine. Lazy. Drifting through lockdown.

I do have some structure in my life: I cook, I continue my Duolingo Gaelic course (even if I don't have a clue how to pronounce most of the new words I'm learning), I write my weekly blog post and I've even resumed my Pilates class on Zoom.

I'm grateful to be here in Dumfries and Galloway in a house with a garden, not stuck in a high rise flat in a city. My gratitude doesn't prevent my emotional responses being all over the place. I become enraged when I read the government is now telling us to clap for the NHS – as if they came up with the idea – and again when I see Police Commissioner Cressida Dick standing on Westminster Bridge like she's attending some kind of street party, with hundreds of people, including many police officers, ignoring the social distancing rules.

While I am full of admiration for Captain Tom and his fundraising efforts, I am appalled we should think it's OK for an old man to shuffle around his garden with a walking frame to raise millions of pounds for the NHS. Will we ever know how that money is spent?

I don't often cry, but tears well up when I hear of people dying alone in hospital, with no family around them. A 17-year-old carer gives a client a gift of a cushion on which is imprinted his late wife's photo. He cries. I cry.

I cry at funerals shown on television where there are hardly any mourners and I cry when I hear sons and daughters speak of their grief at not being able to say goodbye.

I hear of one hospital which is now allowing one family member, in full PPE, to say goodbye at the bedside. I well up when someone says we must talk to our loved ones about how we want things to be done because there may not be the chance once someone has the virus. I look at the DH. We have not had that conversation.

I shout at Health Secretary Matt Hancock, giving vent to my frustration, and my fear. And I think it is OK actually, to be emotional during this weird time.

Pam: **Locked Down in Solitude**

This time last year I was unaware of a place called New Galloway, even though I frequently visited Scotland and had, indeed, worked in Glasgow. Usually I breathed a sigh of relief as I read: *'Fàilte gu Alba'* on my way north. Then, last July, I saw that St. Margaret's Church needed a rector. I applied and the rest is history.

Having moved in mid-November, I was starting to feel at home when, out of the blue, I had a heart attack resulting in six weeks off work. On February 16th I was back in action again, and a month later came lockdown. For me this couldn't have happened at a worse time. As a part-time rector, much of my work focused on our weekly worship and pastoral support, leaving time to settle in and orientate myself to this glorious part of the world. Finding myself locked down, alone, and on the edge of the village, has not been easy though there have been glorious days sitting in the huge rectory garden when I thought I could become a recluse. The thought soon passed!

For me, Covid-19 has proved a time of serious reflection about the nature of church and ministry. I am nowhere near solving the dilemma that our situation poses, but I'm a bit like a dog with a bone; there are days when I bury it, then dig it up and try again.

Things first came to a head on Easter Sunday when I realised I was unable to engage with the holiest day in the church's calendar. I could not reconcile the feelings of pain and, yes, anger at what was happening around the world with any celebration. It was hard to share this because I felt guilty. I couldn't move on from Holy Saturday, the day of deep mourning after the execution of Jesus. Thankfully, through social media, I realised I was not alone.

Then I found a brilliant talk entitled *Crying in Crisis*, which articulated what I was feeling. The tragedy of people dying alone, unable to be held by a loved one, or to clearly see anyone's face, breaks me up, but also reminds me that I am likely to die alone. As a single person with no family there are times when I feel like shouting: "Welcome to my world," to those who are struggling with isolation. I know people are missing their families, but I confess to feeling jealous that they have someone to miss. I feel the guilt piling on me as I write the words rather than just think them. And then I remember that the last words of Jesus at his execution were, "My God, why have you given up on me?" For him and his friends, all they had worked and hoped for was gone. Life would never be the same again. And it wasn't - though beyond the pain they experienced a new way of living.

Will our lives ever be the same again? Do we want it to go back to that 'normal' where so much was going wrong in our world - vast wealth and abject poverty, racial discrimination, climate change - and so much more? A world where so much anger is just below the surface? Where it can feel that we are here to serve the economy, rather than money being simply a man-made tool of exchange?

So many questions flying around, and so few answers. But then, does anyone have any answers. I think not!

Christine: **A Glimmer of Hope**

I thought, along with many other people, that coronavirus would be a fairly short-lived affair, probably confined to China where it first started. Quick and easy global travel brought it here. Many people have lost their loved ones without even having the chance to say goodbye. We have been deprived of our freedom of movement, and there has been a lack of clarity on how to behave which has been irksome.

We seem to have weathered the storm, but unanswered questions still remain. How long is lockdown going to carry on? What will happen when we are finally free of restrictions?

Are our lives going to go back to normal, or will 'normal' be different?

Some people talk about celebrating the end of restrictions, but I think that most of us worldwide will be quietly grateful for still being here. I know that in some cultures, they light small nightlights to remember those who are no longer with us - just a thought...

Cath: **Useful Again**

I've lost track of the weeks since lockdown started and normal life was put on hold. But I've been busy. I started, like a lot of people, to do jobs which I never get round to, lacking both time and inclination. Happily a couple of rooms were cleaned and even vacuumed round the edges, After a couple of weeks, I fell back into my old lazy ways, reinforcing the knowledge that I loathe housework. (I would love a house elf, like the one in Harry Potter.) There would be loads of time now to read the pile of books I haven't started yet, and do some art. Our painting group has a WhatsApp group to share and inspire each other. There are also online activities to keep us amused if we are at a loose end.

Then came a Rotary Club email to my husband about a local sewing group making scrubs for local nurses and carers. I got the details and I was in! I wanted to do something practical to help. More outfits are needed so that nurses and carers have enough to change and wash frequently.

Making the pattern took ages. Downloading, sizing correctly, and printing (37 pieces of A4 just for the top!). These were stuck together and then traced off. It used up all my greaseproof paper, but fortunately we had loads of old computer paper which worked fine.

To begin with, I made some sets of scrubs from bits of material hoarded in my stash. Cotton or poly-cotton was stipulated, to withstand frequent hot washing. I was then asked to make some for the NHS using the officially supplied fabric. I was honoured, but doubtful of my own abilities, as my seams are not always as perfect as they should be. The NHS scrubs need overlocked or French seams, but I've been trying flat fell seams. I hope they pass muster. The material I got is a rather unattractive grey. I don't know which lucky folk will get to wear my efforts!

My tidy conservatory now looks like a bomb site. Scraps and threads lie thick and every surface is covered with sewing paraphernalia.

Our wonderful community council has also been busy, supplying additional activities to alleviate the boredom. This week's project was to make a window display inspired by Balmaghie parish. I had a break from sewing (also helps the backache) and fashioned two gold bird pin-shapes as found in the Galloway hoard.

So I've been busy. My books remain unread, the art stuff untouched. The cupboards still need tidying. I feel I'm busier than ever just now. Crisis? What crisis?

June: **What Will We Remember ?**

My first thought was heroism, such a positive. Heroism is a response to something fearsome and none of us will forget Covid-19. It has filled our days, a stealthy, sometimes deadly attacker. Much heroism has come from facing this virus, but an extra burden has hit frontline workers risking their lives with inadequate equipment. And tragically a higher proportion of Black and minority ethnic workers are dying; people already treated badly by Britain.

We will remember the fear, intensified when friends or family caught the virus; such a shock when a close friend caught it. What about the unendurable memories of those whose loved one died, often alone and with no proper funeral? Given a caring government perhaps they need not have died.

I will remember the cynicism of our government which 'lost' EU offers of PPE because Britain wishes to be independent. I shall fiercely remember that, amongst the mishandling of PPE and the pandemic (Boris missed five COBRA meetings on the subject), Brexit and a detrimental trade deal with the US remained prominently on the agenda. I will remember dismay at no action on a fairer tax system or the climate emergency; no helping victims of domestic abuse and little enough for refugees and rough sleepers; the mayhem for schools and the fiasco of universal credit. And I shall bewail the inefficiency of not using volunteers, who stood ready to help.

We have all felt pervading anxiety, fuelled by secrecy and ignorance. My Vietnamese daughter-in-law was racially abused in a Scottish street, accused of being a Chinese virus-carrier. Early national statistics suggested Galloway had few cases, then suddenly we appeared to have the second highest proportion in Scotland. It would have been wrong to identify villages (they can be spiteful places and elsewhere virus sufferers had been badly treated) but it was a relief when *The Galloway News* started giving numbers for this region; reality instead of rumours. A journalist said, "I have to confess that I'm so frazzled that I can hardly read a tweet without interrupting myself to refresh the news feed."

We surely won't forget the ridiculous: dyeing a lake black to deter visitors. Stay on your couch, a sure way to overwhelm the NHS. Stay at home apart from shopping; a free for all in supermarkets. We will remember stock-piling and waste, fights over loo rolls. It took ages to instate sensible distancing in shops. No sunbathing in parks. No walking a short distance then sitting. Police pursued walkers in the Peak District. It's OK to maintain property, but not to paint a room.

And what about the ironical? Kirkcudbright, epitome of a tourist town, sported notices: 'No Tourists Please'.

We will remember our changes, different for each, but universally huge. We have learnt things. For me, I didn't so much mind losing independence, but found it difficult to be indebted. More painfully I became old. Last year I played tennis, cycled and hill-walked. Now I can barely shuffle down my garden. I am clumsy, my memory has gone, I put things in stupid places, I behave irrationally, I have become anti-social, I hop from task to task - I feel old. Half way through my bedtime coffee there was a sudden hot wetness; I had fallen asleep.

And we will remember the glorious weather and gardening. Yet where is everybody? The town is empty, roads empty, walks empty. Are they really on their couches?

Mike: **Elegy for the Daffodils**

In the early morning sun, I deadhead the daffodils, the frayed remnants of their glory crumbling in my hand, their brief season over.

Had they noticed so unique a spring? No visitors extolling their splendour. No exclamations of delight cast on their bashful heads. No deft swaying to evade the youthful frisbee or grandchild's reckless bike.

This season they have blushed unseen, their sweetness wasted on the deserted air.

At the compost heap I scatter their faded fragments. Dust to dust. A blackbird offers benison.

Of course they will flourish come another spring, in glorious, golden resurrection.

Witnessed by whom?

Margaret: **Remaining Quietly in my Room**

Man's unhappiness arises from one thing alone: that he cannot remain quietly in his room. Pascal (1623-1662)

I remember why I wrote that down. Every year I go - went - on retreat to get a little peace. That was when I was reading Pascal, in my little room looking out on the cherry blossom in the monastery orchard. Back then I longed to stop whizzing about, to have time to watch the daisies grow and reflect on the meaning of life. Solitude is something one would always like to have a little more of. Loneliness, on the other hand, is something many people would like a hell of a lot less of.

I could remain quietly in my room for the rest of my life. The Secretary of State for Health tells everyone over 70 that maybe they'll have to remain quietly in their rooms forever, and I shout back, 'NO!' I'll risk coronavirus rather than never hug my grandchildren again, never touch my friends, never eat together, never listen to live music, never walk in a park, never take the bus, never climb a mountain, never sit in a café in the sun and watch the world go by. While I'm part of a global initiative to hold this virus at bay and save thousands of lives I'll conform. We're doing this for one another. But the day someone says that people are as safe as they'll ever be, but you old folk must remain quietly in your rooms for your own good, I say NO!

There's no such thing as isolation. We're sitting in the sun when we hear the wail of fire engines tearing along the street. They fade down the Laurieston road. The word passes from garden to garden: wildfire at Mossdale! The sirens sound intermittently all day. Jake, our postie and one of the firefighters, battles it for 12 hours in unseasonal sunshine. The moors are tinder-dry. To the south-west we see brown smoke like the smoke we saw on TV last year in Australia and Oregon. Driving back from a food pick-up in Laurieston, I see fire engines, and crews in protective gear, hot and weary, at the top of the old railway track. I glance westward. A rush of darker smoke explodes upwards. Conifers?

Next evening, when the wind changes, a slow pall of smoke envelops New Galloway. We close the windows. Miles of moorland are burning to ashes. All those nesting birds: one of the last refuges of curlew and lapwing in Galloway. Is that why I saw the golden eagle yesterday, displaced from its moor? I've sometimes swum in Loch Skerrow after a hot walk - so wild and peaceful. We've sat on the broken platform in the sun eating our rolls. Now we watch TV footage of the helicopter gathering water from the loch and spraying it along the line of the fire.

However much I remain quietly in my room, I can still smell the smoke.

April 27th to May 4th

Prime Minister says UK is 'past peak'...

Face covering advised for shops and transport...

Trump suggests disinfectant cure...

100-year-old Captain Tom Moore raises £32m for NHS...

Ann M: How Did it Start?

It feels an age ago, another world. There had been reports of a virus in Wuhan, a province in China. So far away, what had that to do with us?

Then came the news bulletin saying that the province was being locked down. The screen showed a town in chaos, panic, streets full of people, baton-wielding authorities. We saw a close-up of someone being arrested, wrenched from a group to be isolated. The face was terrified, eyes pleading, screaming entreaties while fighting to resist. Abruptly the camera moved on, but left me with an image I cannot forget. That's how they do things over there, I reflected. I thought of the cameraman, as such brutality is not what China likes the outside world to witness.

Relentlessly the news went on, foretelling how the virus might be counteracted. Still, here in a bubble of tranquility and pregnant sheep it could not spread to us.

I felt grateful I had grown up in the war, although too young to realise the things that were missing. Restrictions, lack of travel and rationing were the norm. I greatly admired my parents and how they had coped, knowing how their life was changed, and the total uncertainty of all things. If we had come through all of that, we'd do the same now. I retired into my bubble.

Lockdown came. And with it a national change, somewhat like the weathercasters when they try to make the best of a bad forecast. A surge of helpfulness has flooded out to every door. I felt put out at being bracketed in an age group at risk. If the only way to help was to keep the rules and out of the way, I'd do it.

Days follow days with little to identify one from another. Statistics and news prove unreliable - as they are apt to do.

Friends and family are hugely important and keep up morale. Children and grandchildren have most to worry over. Chatting to one, marooned in London working from home, she commented it was rather nice not always rushing hither and thither, noticing so much more, and doing things there used to be no time for. I quoted W. H. Davies, 'What is this life, if full of care...' As she did not know it, I laboriously emailed the rest of the poem.

That evening there was no vestige of a cloud. I went out to look at the sky. It was glittering with stars, so bright, so close, seeming near enough to touch, a dome just resting above my roof. Happiness comes quite suddenly and unexpectedly.

I fear now restrictions being eased too soon, of losing what so unimaginable a price has been paid to gain.

Ann G: **Time to Spare**

I like to be occupied with interesting projects. My job, when I worked, kept me fully engaged and I think I realised, even then, it gave me a cast-iron excuse not to prioritise housework. Increasingly, over the years since retirement, our involvement with the organisation Local Initiatives in New Galloway and the Town Hall still gave me plenty of excuses for being busy.

But now there's time to spare. Time to spare! I'm just not used to the idea at all. What does it even mean?

I'm very good at lists. 'It's on the list' has been my way of holding anxiety at bay. Too much to do. Well, at least if it's on the list, it hasn't been forgotten and I'll get there sometime. I still do lists in retirement. In fact, as memory becomes increasingly unreliable, lists become even more important. Since marrying Bob at the outset of our well-timed joint retirement, however, I have learned that some people have a different approach to lists. I write lists to stop things swirling around in my head. It helps to organise my thoughts. It offers me things to do when I have time – at some point in the future. For Bob, however, a list is there to be instantly tackled.

"Right," he'll say, "what's first?"

When in our new-found locked-down, time-rich environment we thought we might do some spring-cleaning, I wrote a list of what needed doing. At that point, plans laid, I would have been quite happy to sit back and find something else more immediate to occupy me. For Bob, however, I might as well have fired a starting gun. We were off! An hour and a half each morning before mid-morning coffee break, with weekends off for good behaviour and - I can't quite believe I am writing this - we have spring-cleaned the entire house.

I didn't set out to write about that at all. It was the sense of time to spare I wanted to capture. Because, after that busy hour and a half, there's still time. Time beyond lists. Writing, like this, offers a way of making use of those moments. Capturing them perhaps.

I'm often caught, on our daily walk, by the ships on the horizon. I've talked of them before. They sit at anchor. Doing nothing. There's a stillness: a sense of breath being held – a pause – a time-warp into which all manner of thoughts and feeling can flow.

I can't connect these two states – the one of lists and constant occupation and quite another, where my mind, like the ships, is suspended in time. Motionless, without purpose or destination.

Today a mirage – they hung in the air. Surreal!

Cathy: **Chill Out**

What did I do at the beginning?

I defrosted the freezer. Oh, the memories within! The expectation of feeding folk.

When did I make chicken stock? Who was round the table to eat the chicken? Can't remember. More than five years ago? Down the toilet it goes.

Ah! Pizza for Scrabble nights... how many meals out of three big pizzas? I'm still Scrabbling via apps **but it is not the same.**

I don't have to tidy the house, make the food... it's easier and cheaper. **But not as much fun.**

Fish fingers. Hurrah! Only four – smaller hurrah. Quite aged – even smaller hurrah.

Um. Ambiguously labelled leftovers... eg 'veggie soup – not nice'. It wasn't, but I will defrost it - no waste (apart from that chicken stock) in these Covid times. Small tubs of soup. Good. The leftovers of great pots made for gatherings with a memory of the joyful shared discovery of dry-frying cumin seeds to spice up carrot soup. Happy reminders of shared cooking and eating.

What is this? Lentils. What do I do with 500g of frozen lentils of dubious provenance? And a similar one of reconstituted dried fruits? Well out of date. It could be a choice of dying from food poisoning or Covid-19.

I hope that two packs of puff pastry for quick communal inventa-meals will last. I could give them away. They are packaged so should be safe. Compared to not-very-nice-home-made soup.

Well, the frozen peas will be OK.

As I hope we all will be when we are round my table again.

Mags: **Transported to Spain**

I've never been disciplined at writing. It flows with urgency or it rests behind the walls of the dam. The experience of the past few weeks has been inexpressible.

Here I sit in all the comfort of my lovely life while families in the cities are crowded together, children unable to play out of doors. It seems like a sci-fi horror film. Thousands of people dying. Thousands of dedicated NHS and care workers struggling on in unimaginably difficult circumstances. Women trapped indoors with screaming toddlers or abusive partners, or both. To see Boris clapping for the NHS workers before he was ill made me sick with fury, knowing how under-resourced they are. One can only hope his experience in intensive care has changed the man.

Meanwhile this lovely weather has transported me to Spain, where I lived for a couple of years. I dug out some old clothes that have strong memories woven within. I have my 10.30 *carajillo* (coffee and brandy) sitting in my lovely sunny corner surrounded by those wild violets. This Spanish habit was quite normal. At 6.30 in the morning on my way to work I would stop for breakfast where the men would be sitting at the café bar, blue-overalled, with glass and cup in hand, conversing loudly. Here in Scotland this consumption of alcohol would break the sun-over-the-yardarm restriction. Ah well, changed times, changed lifestyle. The sun has clearly made a difference to how I experience this weird world we find ourselves in.

I'm unable to work in the garden this year due to missing the boat with hip replacement surgery and other limitations on my ageing back, so it's interesting to watch the garden doing its own thing. Dandelions are now welcome among the daisies in the grass: no lawn, this patch of green. Pretty new wild flowers, which in previous years would have been removed during weeding, are finding their place.

Many of us have written of the bubble within which we find ourselves. Perhaps others too have a bubble within this common bubble? I am quite absorbed, in my medicated bubble, by my intention to stay mobile and sane while we await the 'new normal' which will emerge. Perhaps my restricted situation is a blessing in these circumstances? My losses are fewer.

Leonie: **Wildlife Garden Journal**

My garden, created from a furze-covered knowe, supports many of the original wildflowers.

Lady's smock *Cardamine pratensis*
emerges as the cuckoo comes,
wearing not so much a smock
as an under-slip, lilac, silky
over pale limbs to seduce
the orange tip butterfly.

Herb-robert *Geranium robertianum*
adaptable, propped against the wall

to lift pink, carmine-streaked flowers
or, like a starfish, spreads across the ground
robust, rhubarb-red stems with glistening hairs,
rank, ferny leaves that repel flies, make a balm
for wounds and housemaid's knee.

Primrose *Primula vulgaris*
under hedge or woodland edge
pale lemon herald of spring
pin-eyed or thrum-eyed
a delight to behold.

A browse through *Flora Celtica* demonstrates that our ancestors must have tested nearly every possible plant for its medicinal properties. We are still at it. My thoughtful brother, worried about my solitary lockdown, insisted I purchased Bach Rescue Remedy (other brands are available). Contents: flower essences in a grape alcohol solution (sounds quite like wine to me): rock rose, impatiens, clematis, star of Bethlehem and cherry plum. I bought it to calm him down.

Ros: Sundowners Part 2

With Malcolm, a great lover of all animals, and Crispy the lamb asleep together on the kitchen floor downstairs, I lie awake in bed caught in a tangled and tender web of sleep-defying anxieties and ethical quandaries. My eldest daughter's question, in response to the cute picture of Io-and-lamb I'd gaily emailed out to family: "isn't that stealing?" (Eve can always be relied upon to stop my whimsies dead in their tracks, sometimes with no more than a raised eyebrow.) There's a realisation that this small creature, which now looks set to bloody well live, will require round-the-clock mothering for at least the next few weeks. This at a time when I am already stretched to my limit working from home doing the world's most un-interruptible job, while looking after a seven-year-old child. The shame of having made an unwise snap decision based on nothing more substantial than spontaneity and sentimentality. The possibility that I may, indeed, be complicit in theft - or, worse, have transgressed some unspoken country code of conduct into which I had never been initiated, and of which I have now blunderingly revealed my ignorance.

These threads dance and chatter through my mind as I lie there not sleeping. It's startling how thin your skin gets when you retreat from the world.

At 8 in the morning, my friend phones me. "I'm going to talk to the farmer and confess my deed," she says. "I'm feeling I've made a mistake." I say I've been feeling a bit funny about it too. We talk briefly but expansively, in broad brush strokes, touching on modern farming methods, and globalisation, and attachment theory, and what it feels like when people think you're mad, before coming to a clear consensus about what we need to do next. I love these moments, when you remember exactly why your friends are your friends.

Half an hour later, we are perfecting our bottle-feeding technique. I'm clasping the lamb tightly to my chest, Malcolm is tilting the bottle just so. Io is standing in front of us in a shaft of morning sunlight, enjoying the two of us sharing stories about how we had to hold her just like this when she was born a month prematurely, was still too weak to latch on to the breast - and now look at her, so tall and strong and covered in freckles and with a mouthful of new grown-up teeth! We see my friend waving outside our kitchen window. We bid the lamb a fond farewell, and Io has a five-minute gut-wrenching sob in my arms.

Later, my friend texts: "All's well that ends well. The farmer returned the lamb to the ewe and Crispy latched on! So it really is the Adventures of Crispy: what a wee survivor, and thank Io for looking after Crispy so well."

This lucky escape from a romantic idea that could so easily have become a reality of burdensome and inescapable responsibility leaves me feeling light as a feather and filled with gratitude, both for this magical and slightly surreal interlude, and for its impermanence.

I decide that from now on, I'll save my drinks for sundown.

Gordon: The Bigger Picture

The desire to find someone to blame disregards what we have done to make the pandemic possible: relentless expansion into wild spaces; astonishing levels of air travel; chronic underfunding of the NHS; an economy running on fragile supply chains; social networks that rapidly spread misinformation and the devaluation of expertise. Before it happened very few would accept that we had built a world prone to a pandemic, but not ready for it.

We need a James Bond type who survives successive trials and eventually heroically rescues the world. If such a character exists in this pandemic, they need to be not an individual, but the entire modern world. The end of the journey and the nature of its final transformation will arise from our collective planning and action. Are we capable of doing that? What can an ordinary individual do? Each to his own. As a scientist and author, I am writing a dystopian novel encompassing climate change, corruption and, yes, pandemics. But there must be more of us to do things to get a movement going.

My mobility is improving fast so now a little gentle running. Lovely in this weather. Little traffic, birdsong, lambs frolicking, leaves and bluebells out, a few others walking or cycling. Wouldn't it be great if we could keep the good aspects of the lockdown? This view is taking hold in places, but the pressure to get back to the old normal is very powerful.

Lynn: **Has Lockdown Affected Me? Oh, I Don't Know.**

OK - as far as I'm concerned it's official. Well, maybe semi-official, because who's around to tell me it's not? Over these last few weeks of lockdown I realise I have morphed into the archetypal 1950s housewife. Although I don't possess the starched and ironed frilly apron, in every other way my 'out-of-body me' has been observing the change and whispering some pretty unpleasant comments in my good ear, like 'Uh-huh' and 'Oh yeah' as she raises an eyebrow and nods her head in an esoteric fashion.

Absolute proof of this transformation came to me this morning as I was taking the newly-baked banana loaf and walnut bread (both beloved recipes from my dear departed mother's handwritten cookbook) out of the oven.

While they had been toasting away in a glorious 180 degrees C, I had spent a goodly part of that hour washing up the bowls and the measuring cups and spoons. When I'd dried and put everything away, I suddenly remembered I have a dishwasher. What was going on? A month ago I would have bunged every single item on to its shelves and sat down to relax with a coffee. For heaven's sake it stands right beside the sink – and yet I actually washed everything by hand! Not only that - I sang 'Shrimp boats are a-comin'...' at the same time! And, I remembered all the words... how sad is that?

Telltale signs began to show about a week ago when I suddenly became obsessed with polishing brass. When friends, whom I now appear to have alienated, would call to enquire how I'm coping, I couldn't stop boasting about how much brass I had been polishing. I kept turning the conversation around to, well, how much brass I had been polishing. For some reason I couldn't seem to focus on any other topic.

"I've polished all the stair rods" (as if they were interested). "Yes, all nineteen of them!" I went on to tell them about the brass-topped Indian table; how I had used a toothbrush to remove all the crusty Brasso that had accumulated in its grooves over the last few dozen years. Were they bored? Uninterested? Well, yes. Everyone started making excuses to get off the line, like, "Oh dear, I think my cat is on fire" or, "Oops, here comes the cavalry. Bye-ee." Then I started on my fireplace surrounds and the coal scuttle and the fire irons. It just spiralled from there. I prowled the rooms seeking out bits of brass. When my neighbour texted me to say he was going shopping and could he get anything for me, I immediately replied, "Yes, a can of Brasso, please."

He obliged, saying, "I hope this is what you wanted. I've never heard of it before." Humph! He's young. And he probably hasn't got any brass in his house.

I've nearly finished the latest can of Brasso, so I've taken myself in hand. No more polishing brass. I'll simply ignore the two sets of fire irons that are standing in a perfect line like a couple of marines, awaiting their turn for a rub down.

Instead, I've collected the bits of silver that decorate our mantelpieces: they are now waiting patiently on the kitchen table for their turn to shine. I'm certain when this lockdown is over, anyone who comes to visit will have to keep their sunglasses on because the brilliance will be so fantastic they'll go blind otherwise.

Right - where are those Marigolds?

Roger: **Thoughts in the Time of Covid**

Lockdown is comparable to how activists like Camus, author of *The Plague*, experienced the occupation of Paris between 1940 and 1944. Camus thought that the longer the occupation went on, the greater the pressure to take action. Not to be passive and accepting of the circumstances, but wanting to be responsive to all that was happening.

Human experience can be difficult, as I discovered during my years in Palestine and Bangladesh. Helen Dunmore's *Candle Poem* provides the images needed for the UK today:

> *A candle for the crowd around a coffin*
> *and the terrible depth it has to fall*
> *into the grave dug for everyone,*

How to represent the deaths of so *many*?

UK death numbers signify a neglect that has gone on too long. Perhaps at last a candle for an awakened conscience?

Withdrawal from the world to the garden is not the action of choice anymore. There is more to do in the world than just live in it.

If you're over 70 like me how are you perceived? As if ready for the men in white coats to come running across the fields? Am I ready to be defined as an object to which certain characteristics can be ascribed? I am judged by my fitness. One medic referred me to another as 'fit man of 72'. In my eighth decade I take an interest in our world. This life is what I have and I try to understand it.

Christine: **Simple Gifts**

This morning there was an article in the church newsletter by a Capuchin priest from Italy, talking about the changes there. How the sky was a stronger blue and, because there was little traffic noise, you could hear the birdsong. I suddenly realised he was right. I could hear the birdsong this morning. I took pleasure from standing there with Jack, and listening. Not a car around. I could look over towards the hillside and see the new green on the trees and thought how beautiful the countryside looked. It is a great shame that it takes something so dreadful to make you aware of what beauty we have around us and how we don't often take, as W.H. Davies said, 'time to stand and stare'. I shall in future take his wise counsel to heart.

June: **Disjunction**

The disjunction between my life and media news is bewildering; it's difficult not to feel guilty with so much suffering. But I am not staying on my couch. Those were bad, urban instructions; folk need vitamin D and should be outside frequently in the sunshine, abiding by physical distancing.

When hunter-gatherers first turned to farming maybe they felt as I do now: observant and knowledgeable about wildlife but ranging widely until suddenly, with a restricted range, starting to see things differently. In the garden in magical spring weather, I'm seeing and hearing more. Birds stand out. Alone, in the peace, I feed them and they have become tame. I lunch near a bird bath; a bit ill-mannered being fascinated by their ablutions but they seem uncaring. What gusto! Two blackbird baths empty the bowl. Takes just one pigeon. I have spied on nine species and many others come to drink, thirstily.

Unlike my garden, others along the High Street have good nest sites; my one good conifer - the thrushes' tree - died. In drought, when ground hardens, worms go deep. I provide more food but blackbirds cannot use feeders and crows, gulls and pigeons gobble any ground food. A blackbird pair added the top of my garden to their nesting territory and a second pair claimed the bottom half; both repelled invaders. When I began spending all day in the garden and spreading ground food, an interloper male discovered that staying close to me avoided attack from the warier owner. He used to fly to the bird bath, drink, then sing from its edge (blackbirds normally sing from territory boundaries). I 'sang' back and we duetted. His mate then became bold, both came close for food and they managed to rear their brood, despite frequent attacks from the territory owners.

Swallows have declined alarmingly; ours disappeared the day Bryan died. Blue tits nest in neighbours' gardens but feed with me.

Since lockdown I've realised different species take their turn to start singing. Song thrushes were among the earliest, then robins, blackbirds, tits chuntering away in the background. Then suddenly dunnocks. Chiffchaffs arrived, mighty wrens started, now greenfinches. Similarly, there were early insects, a succession of different bees, then flies, beetles and now orange tips. I marvelled at the exotic green creature on my shoe. Then the mesmerising opening of flowers and trees.

It began with endless time, few weeds, too early for vegetables, the dry lawn not growing; a chance to be in control. But stir the soil and tiny weeds awaited rain whilst ground elder knows no check. Apple trees are solid pink, tiny gooseberries and blackcurrants hang prolifically. I earth up the potato sack and broad beans look convincing. I shall mind being kept inside by the rain, but the garden and birds will love it. Blackbirds love singing in the rain.

Meanwhile people continue to die from the shambolic response of this Government. Vietnam with a border with China, a population one and a half times larger than ours and spending a ninth of what we spend on health, has apparently had no deaths because they were prepared with adequate equipment and acted immediately. After two weeks' lockdown their restrictions are largely lifted. I know it's a repressive regime and can you trust their figures, but the source is an excellent long piece in *The Nation*, by George Black, a New Yorker, writing a book about the effects of the American war in Vietnam.

Meanwhile people in the UK die from the shambolic response of our government.

Katy: **Slowing and Shallowing**

My husband settles into a new rota of working long shifts, then having a few days off. I love our quiet time together when he's home. My husband bakes bread, I work on an etching, we ride our bikes and dream of getting a dog. In the small shed at the back of the garden, someone has left old, cobwebby deck chairs and a table. We take them out almost every day to enjoy the sun. The gardens belonging to our terrace are unfenced and we talk to our neighbours far more than usual, appreciating the company.

Food Train are looking for volunteers and I immediately sign up. I hope I don't seem too desperate. I join the shopping team - we are all women - and go around the supermarket collecting items from lists. New rules make it more challenging: a one-way system, no backtracking, stay two metres apart from others. They have put tape all over the floor to define boundaries and when a member of staff tells me I have overstepped my line, I apologise quickly. Some of the shelves – the ones for pasta, flour, toilet roll – are sucked dry. It is a disconcerting sight.

One day, in this beautiful spell of sunny days, we cycle to Kippford as I want to be near the sea. The tide is out and I clamber over the rocks, taking lungsful of fresh air. I find a promising rockpool with two snails moving their tentacles and beckon my husband to watch. We squat for a while, entranced, until I notice a different movement. It's a tiny crab, and when we look closely enough, our faces practically touching the surface of the water, we can just make out a wonderfully patterned shell, dark with small specks of light. But as we watch, it comes undone. Like someone carefully stepping out of a ball dress so as not to ruin it, the creature steps out of its shell and leaves it, now colourless and used, waltzing with the breeze. I feel elated to have witnessed this; a reminder that life goes on, that the world keeps turning. Here in the shallows, a tiny crab has reached a huge milestone, oblivious to the virus wreaking havoc above.

But as we cycle out of Kippford, we are jolted back to reality. Someone has painted a huge sign in red, angry letters and propped it up on an old fishing boat for all to see: '2ND HOME OWNERS, SHAME ON YOU. GO BACK 2 CITY.'

One evening, we sit down to rank my husband's job preferences. I don't want to leave – I love this place I call home. But he can't complete his training here. We rank every region, knowing we could feasibly end up anywhere, or perhaps nowhere. It's like an unfun version of 'would you rather?' Would you rather be in Hull or Nottingham? Would you rather have no hills, or no sea? Be near friends or family? Your family or my family? Eventually, the task is done and we hand our fate over to a computerised matrix. All we can do now is wait. I have plenty of time for that nowadays.

Carol: **The Potting Shed**

There is dirt beneath my fingernails
Good earth
Fetched from rotted heaps,
Cleaved from the mountain
Of last year's growth
The smell is healing balm
To frazzled senses
And smooths away the turmoil
With its promise of fresh green life

My hands are plunged
Into moist, fertile soil
I dive into its bright brown ocean
Feeling at once
At one.
My sense of nurturing returns
With each seed planted
Each shoot emerging
There is life
It will go on
The earth knows it

Rose: **Cup Half Empty**

Each day is the same. I go to bed earlier. I switch out the light because I've had my fill of the day. There's a world out there full of fear and grief. I feel it in my heartbeat when I lie down. I wake up early, my mind whirring. I may as well get up. It's always worth it. The misty light over the field as the sunlight seeps into the day.

I could wear the same clothes every day – there's nothing to dress for but I decide it's important to get out of my pyjamas in the morning. I'm exercised by how I look on Zoom - try to change the camera angle, capture an interesting background, brighten myself up a bit. I look old, like my mother. Annie asks: "How's your hair?" We laugh over the phone, comparing notes on our lockdown locks. How will we look when we emerge, blinking, into the new normal?

I start with a morning walk in the woods. The haze of bluebells spreading out under the trees. The vibrant green of the beech seedlings unfolding underfoot; starry celandines face the sun; shy wood sorrel bows its head and wood anemones drift elegantly. Each day is different. The spidery stitchwort is the latest entrant, accompanied by the unfurling crozier. I take the opportunity to pause by the burn and to listen – water, movement, birdsong. Stillness. I drink it in.

Yesterday as I walked along the path, my tears welled up and ran down my face. Ambushed by loss, I'm grieving a world that goes on without me. It feels childish to be petulant while I'm haunted by images of people trapped in abusive lockdowns. Women and children are dying.

Mustn't grumble, I say. I now have all the time I ever wanted. Thing is, I haven't ticked anything off the list. I'm going to come out of lockdown with mucky windows and old photos still jumbled in a drawer.

This is my time for learning how to be present in the moment. Opportunity disguised as loss. I pull a rune from the bag – The God Odin. The unknowable is in motion. I hold close to the notion of total trust, of willingness and permitting, as I launch myself into another day of lockdown. Each day is the same but different, mustn't grumble.

Cup Half Full

They say that wherever you go, you take yourself with you. I am no different under lockdown than I was before.

But I have had glimpses of the woman I thought I might become, moving from inner-city Sheffield to the green hills of Galloway. I saw her walking down the road the other day, bold in pink and orange. She was swinging a basket to forage for wild garlic in the woods. When I remember to pay attention, she's there, walking through the woods, and sliding into the chilly water. Shells have been found tucked in the moss of the fairy tree. She spends the day making an origami guitar from a dollar bill. At Easter she filled egg boxes with painted stone eggs nestled in tissue paper. She sorts through the bags of old wrapping paper that clutter up the front room. A Galloway landscape collage appears in the cottage window, crowned with a gleaming foil rainbow. Tears roll down her cheeks as she makes nettle soup, joining in a Zoom gospel session, singing on her own, with hundreds of other people. She lights the stove in her shed and disappears down there all morning, immersed in writing. Some evenings she can be found there with a glass of wine and guitar, lit by tropical fairy lights. Sometimes it's hard to see her, I forget that she's there, but I can feel her presence drawing closer as the world I've known falls away.

May 4th to May 11th

30,000 UK deaths:
highest in Europe...

UK nations diverge
on relaxing lockdown...

New car sales
down 97% on year...

75th anniversary
of V.E. Day...

Mike: The Start of the Journey

You step out of the cool dark tenement close into blinding light. Privet hedges exude a dusty heat. Litter lies listless in a molten mirage. August. Glasgow. The sun is shining, the sky is blue, you must get out there and enjoy yourself - mustn't you? There are too many people, too much noise. Frenzy and petrol fumes reek the air. You return to the flat. Trapped.

You imagine being driven back indoors, not by a freak day of heat, but by some debilitating illness or crippling injury, by natural disaster or government edict. You must escape.

That was in the early 2000s. The sentiment was decades older.

You are struggling in the heat up the hill to Station Square. (The hill, if you go there now, is no longer steep; the station long gone.) Your mother and father each carry a case. You have a knapsack with favoured toys. Your father in his sports jacket and flannels stops to wipe his brow - frequently. The cruellest day of heat in the holidays. And you are going home.

You step into the cool dark station booking hall, the sunshine filtered through tall narrow windows, their red and blue glass panels invoking the ecclesiastical. The train home to Edinburgh leaves from the far platform. Was that the year you were escorted, daringly, across the tracks because a runaway train had wrecked the footbridge? Or was that another year? Your myriad memories of the annual Callander holiday collapse into a jumble, a photo album spilt across time.

"Listen," says your father, "listen to the rails." They hum to the rhythm of the approaching train, coasting down the Pass of Leny. A whistle sounds, smoke surges above the trees. Suddenly the Midland 'Black 5' and its maroon coaches are gliding into the station. You are, as always, thrilled by steam's drama. But heartbroken too, as always, on the last day. Farewell to the freedom of roaming woods and riversides, lochside picnics and pottering in streams.

Whistles, shouts in the angry heat, doors slamming, fragments of argument and infant cries, a hiss of steam and with gathering speed the familiar landscape recedes. In tears, you declaim, "I don't want to live in the city. I am going to live in the country."

"Of course," say your parents. "When you grow up you can live wherever you want." And you return to the top floor flat, where, at your bedroom window, if you stand on tiptoe, you can just see the tops of the trees in the park, and think of the woods on the Callander crags.

A succession of cities follows. Edinburgh, then Glasgow. In Helsinki the forest runs up to your flats. "Just follow that path," you are told, "and you will reach Lapland." But Liverpool, not Lapland, follows, then other cities and then, from Glasgow, the leap.

More than half a century after that railway declaration, you leave the city. By that time you have a gnawing fear, an ever-present apprehension that some ill-defined calamity will trap you in a tenement flat, up flights of stairs, behind a door, no grass to step on, no trees for shade, dependent for human contact on a crackling entry phone. 'Lehman Brothers' is in the news. The banks threaten to domino and the world to panic. You move.

You open the new front door on day one. You leave the packing cases half-emptied and take two steps into the garden, wildly overgrown. In a tumble of cries and aerobatics the rooks see off an intrusive buzzard. The birch tree rustles in the breeze above a bloom of wild geranium. The back gate opens to fields, woods, river, hills. You know in your bones that if affliction befalls, this is where it could be tholed.

Leonie: **Wildlife Garden Journal**

Into the lockdown silence, a flood of songs, calls and conversations:
a magpie's harsh 'chak, chak' provokes the mob's staccato chorus.
After many attempts, they see him off, never to return.

A west wind creates a blizzard, a spindrift of pale pink petals;
silently a small white flies on through the storm.

Above the endless sparrow chirping comes the longed-for twitter
of the swallows' return. They flutter, chatter, inspect the shed,
pick an old mud nest, make themselves at home.

At dusk, bats wait for the bounce back of high-pitched squeaks
beyond my hearing, to home in on insects flying above the trees.
A rustle in the undergrowth may be the hedgehog that leaves
black scats on secret trails in her hunt for snails, garden and banded.

Today the last of the migrants arrives, a screaming party of swifts,
giving me the lift I need. Thrush and blackbird sing late songs from high
posts, sweet sounds released by lockdown silence.

Anna: **Rural Lockdown**

Having spent most of our lives in Glasgow and Edinburgh, we
have chosen to live in the Glenkens for the beauty and tranquillity of
the place. Lockdown has made very little difference to our lives, except
we no longer shop in Castle Douglas once a week and miss our operatic
visits to the Fullarton or dinner at one of our local restaurants. Our new
neighbours have been a tower of strength, doing my supermarket shop

for me. We reward them with a glass of wine in the garden, observing social distance, of course.

We are very fortunate in that we have beautiful forest walks on our doorstep. On Monday I asked my gardeners to take an old wooden bench down to the loch half a mile away. My husband is unable to walk very far these days due to a heart condition. Yesterday was our 49th wedding anniversary. I made up a picnic lunch with bottle of wine and drove half way to the loch. We walked the remaining quarter mile to the water's edge and enjoyed our picnic in fine weather. It is quite a few years since my husband last visited this spot - he much enjoyed the experience!

I think the pandemic will have an effect on how we all conduct our lives from now on. Gone are the days of shaking hands, hugging and kissing everyone, sometimes even strangers: a practice observed and adopted from continental visits; in the past, British people did not indulge! Local authorities could introduce one-way pavements, with walking on the right-hand side, facing oncoming traffic and, of course, we will have to observe social distancing for a long time to come.

I do feel very sorry for people cooped up in flats, especially during this fine weather. My younger son and his wife are both working from home and attempting to home-educate their two girls. They are finding this quite onerous - early morning starts and working till late at night, although one advantage is they do not have the complications of commuting and taking the girls to and from school.

This virus was imported to our country. People on incoming flights, boats, trains should have been required to self-isolate for two weeks on arrival. It is unbelievable that many weeks after lockdown, three flights a day were still coming into Edinburgh Airport from Italy. Lifting lockdown completely will be another mistake as it is going to take at least a year to make any substantial difference. Mind you, I can see nothing wrong with taking my husband for a drive to a remote cove on the Solway coast for a picnic!

He has made lunch!

Mary: **A Bad Week**

For the first time since lockdown I'm feeling constrained by the restrictions and worried about the future. As a nation, we have willingly given up almost all our civil liberties to stop the spread of the virus and prevent deaths. Are we going to spend the next few years trying to win back those rights and liberties? And don't forget Brexit.

Sultan emails from Afghanistan to tell me Caca (Uncle) Qurban died today, not from Covid-19 but from cancer. I knew it was going to happen, but it is still a shock. He was a good friend. For some reason, a scene keeps replaying in my head of him teaching me the Dari word for matches. And the game he played at Afghan 'ceilidhs' (same as Scottish ceilidhs but with tea instead of whisky) using a matchbox, which ended up with us all, including him, falling face down on the carpet.

I truly, if foolishly, thought we would meet again. I want to go and climb Screel in his memory (we were going to climb Koh-i-Mich together one day) but I can't. I want to go to the coast. I miss the sea. I want to go to the garden centre and buy colour and scent for my garden. I want to hug my friend in Glasgow who has spent years building up a community arts organisation and feels as though her life has been blown apart.

At least Jawad sends some positive news from Afghanistan. He has secured 30,000 euros to supply soap, PPE, thermometers, and sanitising liquid for 500 families in which there is TB, and another 90,000 euros to provide food for 1,500 returnees from Iran. He even sends me photos of the staff in their protective kit using those very fancy thermometers which always make me think of stun guns. In the meantime, the president (well, one of them as Afghanistan has two at the moment) has ordered the distribution of 'one bread' to be given to the poor people, this despite being given thousands of dollars in aid. It makes me wonder who is making a fortune out of Covid-19 here.

And will our civil liberties ever be restored?

Ann G: **Virtual Reality**

My youngest grandchild lives in a little cottage with a big, exciting garden and a daddy working from home just now. He has an attentive, playful mummy and a daddy who engages him in gardening, chopping wood, walks and driving him around on the ride-on mower. He has just turned three and in many ways it's an ideal situation.

But before lockdown, he loved his little friends. He had just started at playgroup, enjoyed rhyme-time at the library and toddlers' group. He tells me sadly on FaceTime that everything has closed - the shops, the library, the cafés, the play parks. He cries bitterly after they arrange an online playdate for him because it's not real. He wants to be able to hug his best friend. Virtual reality just doesn't cut it.

Reality is a strange concept at the moment for all of us. Seeing him, at three, try to make sense of it breaks my heart. It's funny too, because as well as knowing that seeing people on the screen is no substitute for reality, he's also able to create imaginary worlds where his parents struggle to keep up with his conviction that this will be real.

"Today we're going for a walk to find the Hundred Acre wood and have a picnic with Pooh Bear and Tigger."

"We're going to visit Blippi. We will have to fly on an aeroplane, and I have packed some toys to take with me."

He has too, a big bagful. It's quite a challenge for his parents to negotiate the line between imaginary play and reality so it doesn't end up in a melt-down.

He'll decide that tomorrow it will all be better and everything will be open again, and weep when they have to explain that it won't be over - not yet. He's trying so hard to find solutions.

Yesterday he had an idea: "If I could do a silly dance for people, it would make them smile and laugh and then the virus will go away and everything can open again."

Mummy thought it was a sweet idea and that a little bit of virtual reality fairy dust, involving videoing his dance, might just do the trick.

Daddy thought it was a sweet idea too, but went for the more literal take on the suggestion. And the upshot was, with some trepidation, they drove the couple of miles to Mochrum, where they had lived before and knew a few people. Little one did get to dance, although most people were out for a walk or not answering their doors.

Life trundles along bumping up against tough realities, but the wonders of imagination and the amazing opportunities offered by modern technology do allow some respite too. I cherish the fact that yesterday his nine-year-old cousin, my other grandson, holed up in a tiny flat in London, was able to read him *Mr Topsy Turvy* on a video-call – to the delight of them both. Virtual reality and imagination reign OK! Sometimes.

Lynn: **Games People Play**

For those of us who are fortunate enough to have family, but unfortunate enough not to have them living nearby, communications have certainly become an interesting aspect of life under lockdown. A few years ago my children were scattered far and wide across the globe – one in Japan, another in Germany and a third on the west coast of Canada. It had its plus points; giving us a reason to explore parts of the world we might never have thought of visiting. During that period of family life, both parents were immensely grateful to receive sporadic handwritten letters and the odd telephone call. And so it was. I now consider myself blessed because one by one they have drifted back to the UK and settled down with families of their own.

Living alone in lockdown for just short of two long months, it seems like ages since I last physically embraced any of them. Instead, a social time has begun to take shape within our family that revolves around playing games and having chats on media sites I had never heard of. Skype and FaceTime seemed the ultimate in technological inventions to my mind. Nowadays folk are into Hangouts, and are Zooming all over the place.

We have always been game players. Kahoot is now the quiz site of choice. For the last three Saturdays we have met together with wine glasses topped up and bowls of snacks to hand. We spend the evenings laughing and chattering about all sorts of things while attempting to win the quiz. We tidy ourselves up and the women put on lipstick. I even put on a splash of scent from the last bottle of perfume I ever got from my husband. It's a challenge to create a quiz that participants from age five to 75 can take part in without becoming bored or losing interest. It has worked to distract me from our situation so far.

But oh, how acute is the isolation when my screen shuts down.

June: **Losing Control**

As somebody said, most of us now have time for navel gazing, and it's uncomfortable.

With a mystery killer on the rampage does anyone feel in control? People try, but once control feels out of reach, folk often start drinking, eating, taking drugs, becoming violent, becoming depressed or becoming ill.

Different strategies help. My friend needs tidiness, with every task finished and the pace slowed to fill the time. My neighbour goes beyond that: the same schedule every day, tidy, finished and like new, with lollipop bushes. I take the opposite tack; many projects on the go means 'busy' and, for me, 'busy' gives an illusion of control.

I used to be critical of folk who were bored. How could they be bored in such a wonderful world? But boredom can be a precursor of depression; maybe I made sure to avoid it as part of being in control. An article in *The Observer* made me re-think: John Danckert and

James Eastwood, in their book *Out of My Skull*, say boredom leads to a combination of lethargy and restlessness; turning to easy distractions, like games on our phones, makes it worse. They argue that boredom lays down a challenge to us. "It signals that we are unengaged, in need of an activity to satisfy us. Boredom can steer us towards realising our potential and living full, meaningful lives." They suggest it has led the push towards creativity, innovation and growth.

Pondering this when I woke early, I got up and tidied three rooms, took out my bulging compost bag then ruefully looked at my half-finished projects. A fleece cloche shredded by mice being mended, half-done spring cleaning, ground elder quarter-tamed, shrubs in holding beds, that cementing job, two sheds to sort, editing, a book to write and lots of outside painting.

And why sow enough vegetables to feed Kirkcudbright? And why too early so they're leggy, needing protection from frost and endless watering? Eager birds are waiting for them to become succulent. Sparrows have unpicked the twine holding my pea netting.

Before lockdown, my hairdresser's planned holiday prompted a short haircut. I'm now catching up with everybody else and contemplating the new fashion. A centre parting then let it hang, rather ominously known as 'curtains'. No podiatrist, so I have claws; no cleaning help so no tidying before she cleans. And living alone means no responsibility, no need for schedules, no structure. Mealtimes, what I eat, bedtime, activities, all fluctuate widely and, without my usual pattern of outside commitments, I find I am, alarmingly for me, out of control.

I shall not be bored, but how much lack of control can I tolerate?

Just discovered I have my fleece on inside out.

Roger: **Lost Now**

Noisy diesel, the powerful sound of a locomotive: a crane works on railway repairs. Yellow lighting reveals in black relief the men fixing the railway. On my side of the tall metal fence I see a long line of trees: bright summer colours in daylight, but the magic of the place emerges after dark. Cover is provided by a garage. Astonishingly, I am looking at four indistinct shapes in the light filtering through the trees. Four foxes. It is I who retreat. I guess gardens and dustbins are going to be disturbed.

The foxes improve the environment of traffic-cursed roads and become 'the other'. They ease the oppression of city totality. I'm a captive of the city, but the city was my rescue too. I needed the Queen Elizabeth Hospital for my cancer operation.

My partner, Annie, brought me into her home after my surgery. I am 74 and had lived in Galloway since 2001. Not being in a green place is my lockdown struggle.

Once, the opportunity of weekly returns to the Galloway hills sustained me, but these have been extinguished for weeks now by lockdown. The waking in the morning to anticipate the joy and renewal of time with nature, river, mountain, forest, field, sea… lost now.

What choices are there as lockdown bites? Waiting to know.

Cath: **The New Normal**

Recently I've done loads of sewing, making scrubs for doctors, nurses and care workers. It's been great, feeling useful and pretending that this is normal life. But now I'm waiting for more material and instructions. That is when reality hits home. I'd love to nip into town - trawl round the charity shops, meet my friend for coffee, and lust over the gorgeous stuff in Designs.

Instead, I have made a scarecrow; a community council activity to help our sense of togetherness. Ours wears goggles, but needs more PPE! I also made a banner to mark VE day, and fastened flags to the front railings. With the Galloway Hoard display in the window, the combined effect is somewhat bizarre.

When I've been into Castle Douglas to get supplies, the familiar and beloved shops are now cold and unwelcoming, locked and shuttered. The desolation is compounded when peering in through the mostly stripped windows. All is dark and miserable yet hiding in the shadows lie those interesting and desirable objects which we crave so much.

The mannequins in one shop have been swathed in tissue, presumably to stop the sun from fading the garments being modelled. Or perhaps they are naked and the paper is to protect their modesty! The mannequins looked forlorn and miserable, like the rest of the shops. I miss the hustle and bustle. When people are queueing up outside the few open shops, butchers and bakers, it feels a bit awkward to stop and chat to a known face.

A new etiquette is developing: am I blocking the pavement and how loud do I speak? Discreet conversations aren't possible – comments and discussions must now be acceptable to all within earshot, so feel a bit stilted and superficial. We keep hearing about the 'new normal'. But I love talking to people, and 'mooching'. Will it ever happen in the old way again?

Technology is OK up to a point, if you have the means. But it's exhausting to have meetings and group chats online; much trickier not being able to read body language, witty quips or subtle expressions. There is a basic human need for touch and close proximity. Camaraderie is built in face-to-face meetings. Without hugging and kissing, or even bumping elbows, a pat on the shoulder, sitting close enough to chat across a table or whisper into someone's ear, what are we to do? Will this go on indefinitely? I really don't like this 'new normal'. It's not the lack of activities which is hard; just the dearth of human contact, despite having a husband and son at home!

How much harder for people who live alone and now have to endure social distancing as well. As my daughter, looking after a toddler, said, "I just want to go to the pub!"

So let's raise a glass, and drink to the past, and to the future! Cheers!

Rose: Wake Up! Watch Out!

I bought a diary in February, as an afterthought. I always print out a year planner to plot all my comings and goings: festivals, gigs, rehearsals, workshops. The change of season heralds the arrival of visitors, like summer swallows, wanting to chatter and play, visits to and from family. I constantly check to see where the next breathing space will present. By the end of February, 2020 was pretty full. Booking now for Christmas I'd joke.

I never transferred the information from the planner to the new diary. It's now irrelevant, that year plan of a former life. I did put in the dates for the Cairn Chorus concerts. The pencilled dates float past me as I turn the empty pages. We would be singing at Moniaive Folk Festival this very afternoon, a fabulous programme: *Rise Up Singing* – songs of protest, hope and resistance. Annie was due to be visiting this week, part of her

70th birthday plan. "I suppose we'll see each other again sometime," she says on the phone. I was eighteen when we first met.

My diary now works in reverse – I put something in after it has happened. I note down if I have a phone call or an unexpected encounter: the date I sent my writing off, the rare outing for a safely distanced collection from Sunrise or pre-booked mobile fish and chips. I need a record of what's happened, to keep hold of the pieces of the jigsaw.

I heard retired doctor, Tom Heller, talking on the radio about having Covid-19. He described feeling confused and disorientated, which actually prevented him from identifying his symptoms and seeking help. I recognise my experience of lockdown in what he says.

As I drift through the empty pages of my week I've started to listen out for the quiet news, consumed and buried by the virus. It's business as usual out there. HS2 is on the move destroying the ancient woodlands in its path. I can hear the rumble of capitalism's empty stomach; I sense the beast's impatience to start feeding again. Planes are flexing their wings on the runways, straining at the leash to be up and away. Cars are coming back on the roads.

Wake up! Watch out!

Margaret: **Disjointed**

My friend could not visit
her mother, in the hospital
where she died.
Clutching the phone, I look out
on swirls of cherry blossom
and I remember
exactly
what my friend just lost.

Summoned by Care Call,
foolish in mask and gloves,
I sit by my neighbour.
She lies prone, as she fell.
The ambulance is on its way.
I'm not to touch her.
We talk about gardens.
All I can do is not leave her.

Three tawny-owl chicks
fall from their nest,
speckled lumps of down
on cold ground.
Their mother swoops and calls -
I shouldn't scoop them into my jacket.
Too weak to hold the branch,
By dusk they're dead.

The future is shadows
in an abyss
and can't be changed.
I want to make
everything
be all right
but nothing joins up.
Nothing touches.

Meteor showers blaze
like portents
in a post-industrial sky.
Next morning
I search online.
I can't find
what they are,
only what they are made of.

May 11th to May 18th

Covid-19 death toll exceeds 40,000 in UK.
Quarter in care homes...

Govt borrowing to meet Covid
tops £123 Billion...

New UK Government 'Stay Alert'
slogan rejected by Scotland...

Massacre in Kabul
maternity hospital...

Mary: And We Think We Have Problems

You may have seen or read the news reports of the attack by gunmen on a maternity hospital in Kabul, which took place today. Aqila, a midwife and the daughter of one of my volunteer health worker students, works there. Her sister, Arifa, messaged me on Facebook. In typical Afghan tradition, she did not want to tell me about bad news so sent a photo of herself, her dad and her mum standing under a blossoming cherry tree. Only when I replied did she tell me it had been a bad day and I heard the story.

Aqila sought refuge in the safe room along with several other members of staff while the gunmen fired indiscriminately into the wards in which mothers lay with their new babies.

Arifa, only 17, is trying to comfort her mother, who, she says, keeps crying, and her sister, who is, understandably, in shock. And I'm writing this and wondering how I can have inserted so many commas into one sentence. Thinking of anything other than the photo she sent me of a new mother holding her baby – both dead.

Aqila first contacted me a few years ago to tell me she was a midwife in Bamiyan, the capital of Central Afghanistan. She told me she became a midwife because her mother had been one of my students on a mother and child care project years ago. Seeing the value of education, especially in women's health, she encouraged her daughter to study. Her message gave me a warm glow – a feeling I had done some good.

Of course, now I feel guilty for being an interfering westerner. Instead of cowering in a safe room of a maternity hospital while gunmen went on a killing spree, Aqila might have been sitting at home, avoiding Covid-19 and playing with her kids.

Taliban has denied they were responsible – but has not denounced the attack and killings. One thing is certain, any notion of there being a peace deal has ended. It wasn't a peace deal, anyway, it was something concocted by America and Taliban, without any participation of the Afghan Government. Taliban claimed the deal as their victory. And now, they are showing the world, if only the world would look, what a victory for Taliban means.

As I write this, sometime after midnight here, it's the early hours of the morning in Afghanistan but I know one family who is not sleeping. And on top of this, they, like us, have Covid-19 to worry about.

I'm sorry. I'm not good at keeping bad news to myself, bottling it up. I need to tell someone, talk to people – and tonight you are those people.

Ann M: **Getting Back to Normal?**

What is normal?
Talk of getting back to normal?
Did we like normal? We complained about it endlessly: trains late

or cancelled, overcrowded roads, breathing filthy air, and noise, always noise. Normal is different things in different places. Not everyone can live up here, maybe some wouldn't even want to - midges, rain, more rain. We just know we are the lucky ones who do. I still find it hard to believe what is really happening, confined alone in my age bubble.

Recently I left the bubble to join an outdoor supper, well spaced out, under an incredibly beautiful evening sky. The family dog thrust her nose at my knee. Surreptitiously I stroked her head before she wandered off looking somehow short-changed.

Later on someone was busy knitting. Needles and fingers danced, the moss stitch square grew and was cast off - a perfect dish cloth, firm textured, inviting use. Next day I felt I'd dreamt it all, somehow not been there. Remembering stroking the dog's head, then picking up the cloth and feeling it just as it really was. I realised the oddness was the lack of touch, of contact, of withdrawal maybe.

But those dancing fingers reminded me of watching a spider spin its web; a large spider in the gateway of a game reserve. The new web took several days to complete: fixing silken points, abseiling down, climbing up with this endless thread, no knots or tangles, crossing points secure. This was a place one visited hoping to see the Big Five, but I remember the spider's web.

This morning at 8.40 am two jet planes roared over, shredding the air. We knew that the Ken Bridge was a target on training flights, so this was a reminder of past normal, as is the sight of vapour trails across the sky.

My two-year-old great-grandson has watched seeds germinate and had time to harvest radishes he carefully tended over the weeks while parents worked from home. His grandparents had an exhausting time, but forged a lifelong bond and filled a need. It used to be normal for several generations to live in the same house. Grandparents had a role to fill.

We want, we want, we have had - and now we find out what we need. That's different.

Beverley: **Disaster Strikes**

Today I am supposed to be returning from a long-anticipated Scottish Opera trip to Turin and Milan which was only cancelled three weeks ago. I assume we will get our refund in the distant future.

In the afternoon I go to the loch to swim: a beautiful day, but the air is still cool and the water very cold. On my return, still in a bathing suit with a jumper on top and wearing flip flops, I water my parched garden before settling down to my usual evening at the opera (*Cavalleria rusticana* and *Pagliacci* this evening).

As I wander down the little slope, pulling the hose behind me, my left foot slips on the dewy grass. I crash to the ground, doing the splits, right knee and foot concertinaed underneath me, accompanied by an ominous little clicky ping in my ankle! I lie still for a while, assessing the situation. Do I feel sick? No. Do I feel faint? No. So probably nothing broken. I gingerly crawl up the slope until I am sure I am on the flat. Then I take a deep breath and stagger to my feet. To my relief, I can weight-bear on the right foot and stand upright, but I can't lift either foot off the ground and my right knee and ankle are agony.

Do I have my phone with me? Of course not! The forecast said the temperature would go down to minus one tonight. So not a night for sleeping out in the open, almost naked. I manage to shuffle up the slope, turn off the tap, and get one hundred yards across the gravel to the front door. Fortunately my house is quite small so I can hang on to walls, window sills and doors to get to the kitchen. I get a small plate, a biscuit and a piece of cheese, grab a glass and a bottle of wine and sit in my study to assess the damage. The pain in my swelling ankle and knee is below the joints themselves. So probably a torn ankle ligament and a sprained knee; Ibuprofen before bed is the best way forward. Thank goodness for my First Aid training when I was President of Dumfries and Galloway Red Cross! I settle down to Cav and Pag, wrapped in a rug with my leg elevated. Best way of taking my mind off the pain! In the morning I get a video consultation with my doctor, who gives me a prescription for pain killers and sends a physio up with crutches, who leaves me to get on with it for the six weeks recovery period. Oh dear! Not only am I in lockdown, I am also incarcerated in the house, as my garden is very unlevel and hilly and I can't drive. What a good thing I have a terrace with a beautiful sea view. Amazing how life can change in an instant!

Lynn: Secrets and Surprises

Today has been a productive one in the garden and I'm just about to reward myself with a lovely gin and tonic. But before I have my first sip I would like to relate a tale that makes me smile each time it comes to mind. It shows how a family found its way to cope with the realities of parenting while having to work at home during lockdown: a serious dilemma taken with imagination and good humour: not mine but that of my son and his family. Today I got a message from him rejoicing that 'the charade is over!'.

Let me explain.

My son and his partner have a very busy and curious little redheaded toddler who is aptly named Ember. Ember is one and a half years old. She walks, she smiles and she giggles. She is also exceptionally 'mummy-centric'. And unbeknown to her, she has been the victim of an exceedingly clever ruse.

Ember's mother has been covering maternity leave and working from home since lockdown began; her father has been furloughed. Their home is an upstairs flat in London which does not have a garden, so her parents devised and put into action a plan to deal with their situation.

This has become their daily routine.

In the morning they have a pleasant breakfast together and Mummy says: "Bye-bye darling. Mummy's off to work now." Kisses all around and Mummy heads down the stairs, waving as she goes out the

111

door. Daddy takes Ember into her room to change her nappy and get dressed. Meanwhile Mummy tip-toes back up the stairs and settles in their bedroom for a morning's work. Ember and Daddy play in the living room until lunch.

Later, as Ember goes for her nap, her mother comes out of isolation and has her lunch. She then returns to work and when Ember awakes she and Daddy carry on playing until teatime. Daddy feeds her and begins her bath ritual when, miraculously, Mummy appears around the door. "Hello darling, Mummy's home." Ember is ecstatic to see her and Daddy leaves them together having fun while he begins to cook their dinner.

My son appreciates the fact that he has this opportunity to spend so much time with his little girl, but admits that it is more demanding than he ever appreciated. Today his partner has completed her contract and for a while can be a full-time Mummy.

For the last seven weeks, Ember, the trusting little soul, never once knew or even suspected that her beloved Mummy was in their home all the time working behind the wall.

I do believe that this incident will go down in the annals of our family history providing smiles over years of re-telling.

Gordon: **Long-term Personal Planning**

I've been adapting to the lockdown well but not totally. It's woken me up to habits I've had without realising. Spending too long exploring things on the internet. Getting used to Ros being around all the time. Sometimes I try to tidy and make a pile to throw out. She goes through it and wants to keep most of it. So the pile stays in the middle of the floor for days before creeping back step by step to where it came from. Covid-19 makes us think of the future. We don't need this big old house; it's bad for climate change and our bank account. We've got stuff accumulated over more than 52 years of married life that is choking the house and even filling our four good-sized cellars. Do we downsize? Do we go south to our other property?

That's completely the other end of the scale: a one bedroom flat, currently rented out, close to where we used to live. We still have an office there for looking after my London clients (10 minutes cycle to station, 40 minutes to London) except that there aren't any clients now. The flat is a delightful little pad at the top of a small three-storey block, well away from the road and in amongst the trees but not shaded by them. An old friend lives in the next flat. A long distance footpath, with its annual race that I run, is just out of the back gate. No run this year. The Canal, complete with pub and restaurant, is a couple of fields away. Opening soon, we hope. That little flat is probably worth more than our house in New Galloway! But it would be a shame to leave here. We'd miss all our friends.

Anna: **A New World Order?**

May 7th was the 100th birthday of the oldest member of the Madeiran Royal British Legion which we enjoy supporting when we visit that island. The following day was the 75th anniversary of VE Day. I listened to Radio Scotland coverage from 6 am to mid-day and marvelled at the varying experiences and memories of people living at that time. In the evening we tuned into BBC1; coverage varied from archival newsreels to the excellent concert filmed within the quadrangle of Buckingham Palace. At 9 pm our Queen addressed the nation just as her father had done 75 years earlier. How proud he would have been to see her now, as strong and erudite as ever, in her 95th year. The BBC should be congratulated on providing an outstanding commemoration.

As I write, it is now Sunday May 10th and we will be addressed later this evening by Prime Minister Boris Johnson.

Whatever he says, our government floundered like numpties in the early days of the coronavirus outbreak. Having observed developments in China and Italy, they should have imposed isolation or quarantine and further tracing on all incoming people to our island. We might have restricted deaths to a few thousand people instead of over 30,000 as of today. On Madeira they have managed to contain the virus with no new cases for two weeks now and are lifting most of the restrictions tomorrow. Our government now talks of imposing isolation on incomers from the end of this month in the hope we avoid a second outbreak. Too little, too late!

Mankind has exploited our planet for the last two hundred years. I consider Covid-19 as nature fighting back. Energy from the sun and the moon, if properly harnessed, will provide all the energy needed for the natural world and mankind. We have to learn this lesson. Lately, the whole world has been on the move, with goods being transported from one side of the world to the other, often to exploit tax breaks. Many economies now rely on tourism, hence the growth of airlines and cruise ships which all run on polluting oil. Even when 'normality' returns, I cannot see ordinary people seeking to travel as in the recent past, nor being able to afford so to do. It is time for us all to respect our environment and for countries to become more self-sufficient. I say this as someone who has travelled widely in the past 25 years coming to the conclusion that many places visited were not worth the trouble as home has more to offer.

The time has come to reconsider modern capitalism. It cannot be right that multi-billionaires enjoying the benefits of off-shore tax havens, can furlough their staff in this country and be financed by the British taxpayer. It cannot be right that young men talented at kicking a football can earn twice as much in a week as the average man in a year. I look forward to a new world order where every man, woman and child can live in peace and safety, enjoy the benefits of education, health, clean water and sanitation with a roof over their head and food in their belly.

This should be the coronavirus fall-out.

Mike: **Lock Down - Slow Down**

Six storeys up, a slender steel footbridge across an urban canyon linked our office to the printers. With deadlines approaching, a succession of night editors, 'stone' subs and messengers would scurry over to the caseroom where, amid clamour and mayhem, printers were putting the paper to bed. No zombied ranks at computer screens there: hot metal was still king. We were closer to Caxton than Apple Mac.

As a trainee I'd made frequent sorties over that bridge, always rushing for one reason or another. Then one night, our shift ended, I was crossing with Gilbert, veteran sub-editor and mentor. Gilbert didn't rush.

"Don't look down," he said.

I looked down.

The deck of the bridge was steel mesh: surprisingly large steel mesh. Below my feet, newspaper vans of Dinky proportions queued at the loading bay. Taxis dodgemed their way up the lane. A steady stream of folk was heading into Sammy Dow's. Although I'd never paused to look before, I 'knew' all this was below me. I had arrived along that very lane a few hours ago. I would soon be drinking a pint in Sammy Dow's. But this sudden vertiginous change of perspective, on a world of which I was a part - and yet apart - transfixed me.

With ominous rumble the titanic presses started to roll. The building shook. The bridge picked up the vibration.

"Are you coming for this pint or not?"

I followed Gilbert into the newsroom and we headed for the lift.

- - -

Lock down has led to slow down, and slowing down, I have discovered, is good for your vision. Good for viewing the present world in sharper focus: the order in which trees burst into leaf, the variety of bees pollinating the apple blossom, the strange quadrille as we distance ourselves in New Galloway High Street. But the slow down can also reveal the world we have experienced and life we have lived.

Frequently in these Covid days I find myself pausing, as though on such a bridge again. My mind, given time, randomly rummages the memory banks, producing not sepia-tinted flickers of recollection but vertiginous vistas of vivid intensity with sounds and smells and colours fresh as yesterday. Spend time with your memories and they open like flowers in the sun.

June: **Nostalgia**

I shall have mixed feelings at the end of lockdown. Although, obviously delighted that the virus is receding, I might find it difficult, even with a new hip, to leave my cave.

Thanks to husband Bryan, I have lived in many different countries, always on a shoestring, mostly in huts or tents. During our Galapagos year, we lived in a tent on two uninhabited islands. One was a famous stopover for yachts and we groaned whenever a sail appeared. In lockdown I can feel myself becoming less sociable.

Now with time to ponder I'm feeling nostalgic and often food, with an important role in lockdown, is the trigger.

Ancient soup reminds me of an aversion to my mother's soup, with floating tomato skins and bacon rind.

Once a week I make buttered cabbage with poached eggs. As a teenager, worried about weight, I rejected my mother's sandwiches and bought a cabbage on my way home from school.

Fresh beetroot paired with cheese reminds me of first meeting Bryan. For my 18th birthday my godmother took me to Spurn peninsula and there he was, tall and handsome. Each lunchtime we ate cheese and beetroot sandwiches made by one of the lighthouse wives.

Smoked mackerel with cream cheese and jacket potato reminds me of the Bass and Balcary. We studied gannets on the Bass for three years and the sight and smell of half-digested mackerel on the sides of gannet nests should have put me off mackerel for ever. But caught in Balcary Bay and fried in oats that evening they tasted delicious.

I've never much enjoyed spaghetti, so ignore that bought for my grandchildren. Bryan and I studied relatives of the gannet on the Galapagos and took a year's food, much of it from a ship's chandler in Guayaquil. After a month the spaghetti developed strange black spots; took ages to get enough for supper by breaking out every weevil. We sieved weevils out of the flour too. Apparently weevils secrete a substance that reduces fertility!

Similarly, sardines have been in my cupboard a while. We got sick of sardines after a year.

Bananas seem like a treat in lockdown. We sampled many species from the garden of the world expert in Hawaii, though the tiny, lemony bananas on Fuerta Ventura taste the best.

Picnics have played a large part in my life, from childhood. In this lovely weather I take a lunch basket down to the sheltered part of my garden near the bird bath.

Similarly barbeques. Our family had one with my mother on the beach every Christmas day for 40 years, until she died at 90. I can still see vividly my favourite on Bryan's birthday in Portugal. We built a circle of stones beside a huge, deserted lake. Leaving the meal to cook, we swam with small turtles.

We often had barbeques in the Galápagos; we baked bread in a biscuit tin over the embers, then cooked a huge, freshly-caught crayfish. Afterwards we danced on the sand to Radio Belize. Somehow there doesn't seem much point having a barbeque for one.

Margaret: **Zoom**

Last night my cousins held their Golden Wedding party in London. Einstein would have been quite at home, as time and space collapsed into a curve that might be aptly named Relativity, because it was all about my relations, scattered far through time and space, brought together by Covid-19 in a little capsule hurtling through eternity.

Space: David and Deirdre fill the screen. In a little box at the side are Robin and Liz. I see the portrait of our great-great-grandfather, Simon Halle, hanging above Robin's desk. There's Gerald, immured in his tiny London flat. There are Richard and Margaret in Oxford, Richard sporting a dapper waistcoat. There's Henrietta, looking pale after weeks alone in her flat, but more efficient than we are at Zooming, because she's been teaching on it throughout lockdown: "Margaret, we can't hear you. Press the mute button... bottom left... that's better." There's Caroline in Shropshire, with long hair - it suits her - she's hardly seen another soul for seven weeks. There are Laurie and Jocelyn in Suffolk, and, in a different box, their daughter with a sleek cat on a bed in her London flat. There's Deirdre's sister in Florida. There's her niece, tossing in a yacht in the Savanna estuary. Lucy's in the next box with Michael and their son Benji. Benji is a year old now - he has Lucy's brown eyes... they run in this family.

Time: David continues, "...we recorded our wedding service. Hardly anyone made such recordings in 1970, but Deirdre worked in television... My uncle, Kenneth Elphinstone, took the service. The recording begins with his voice."

My father died on May 16th 1980. It's forty years to the day since I heard his voice. I'm not prepared for this. David might have warned me... Can I even remember? I've tried sometimes, but voices are hard to hear again inside your head. The screen goes black with white lettering: *David and Deirdre Saturday May 16th 1970.*

And then my father: *Dearly beloved, we are gathered here together in the sight of God, and in the face of this congregation...* I am in the face of this congregation. I'm in a little box on a screen which all these people can look at, even the ones I don't know... *it was ordained for the procreation of children...* well, he lived to know his granddaughters.... *For the mutual society, help and comfort...* thank god I'm not alone, listening to this voice so extraordinarily alive out of its time... *or else hereafter forever hold his peace.*

Relativity: This family party was a gift from Covid-19. Like all unexpected and unusual gifts, I don't quite know what to do with it. It's too precious to stick on a shelf and forget. I've asked David for the recording. I'll play it to my father's seven descendants; he would have been proud of them.

My cousins, in their little boxes, are also a gift from Covid-19. If we'd met in London as planned there would have been hugs and kisses, random conversations, personal exchanges belonging only to that particular person. We drank the toast to the bride and groom, each in our box, but the wine wasn't out of the same bottles. You can collapse space and time, but you don't actually touch anybody. My conversations with my father happened in a different key from the one he used in church. I would like to hear his great guffaw of laughter again; no one has recorded that.

Cathy: Crack Up or Lock Down

"How are you?"

"I'm fine. How are you?"

"Oh fine, just getting on with it, no choice really. Aren't we lucky living where we do and having such a good community, and the weather has been marvellous!"

"And it's given us all such an opportunity to do things in the garden…"

But really…

I hate it. I can't bear it, I can't stand it, I don't like it, I can't avoid the dark recesses of my being without other people and going out and adventures and expeditions however small to divert me.

I'm not getting the things done I thought I'd get done and my garden is a jungle.

I am missing the mountains and art galleries and friends and sharing food and…

But I'm fine. Yeah. I hate it and I'll thole it.

And I made a giraffe…

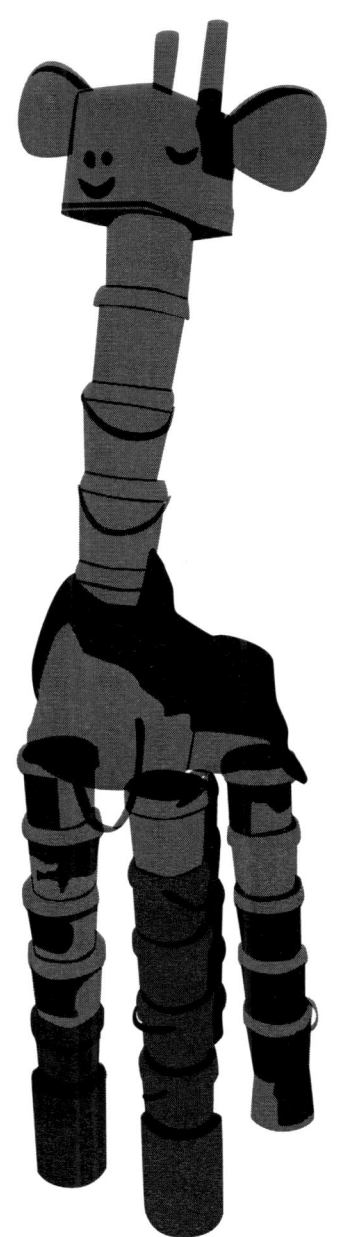

Mary: **Ups and Downs**

It's been a strange week of ups and downs. Events in Afghanistan are, obviously, the biggest down. Yet good things happen there too; things which won't be on the news. A young Hazara man who lives in the UAE and his fiancée who lives in Australia had to postpone their wedding because of Covid-19. They have taken the money for their wedding festivities and, through friends in Kabul, have set up a small project to provide bread to some of the jobless Hazaras in the city.

I'm thrilled when the telephone ordering system at a garden centre works and a delivery of bedding plants arrives. A definite 'up' moment.

I'm not sure about the next one – an up or a down? I'm now eligible for my state pension. When they wrote to tell me, they said I didn't need to take it right now and could defer. Cheek! As I would have received it six years ago if they hadn't kept changing the retirement age, there's no way I'm letting them hang on to my money any longer. It's a definite up to know some money will be going into my bank account each month. It's a down to accept I am now classed as old. Still, I'll be entitled to concessionary fees and fares and a winter heating allowance – if such a thing still exists after this is all over and the country is broke.

I can't begin to picture what life will be like after Covid-19. Will there even be an after or will this virus persist for years to come, or will other, more deadly, strains follow on? Are we entering the beginning stages of a dystopian future? A few weeks ago I was more hopeful the pandemic would lead to a fundamental shift in society, we'd be kinder; and in politics they'd be honest, maybe actually work for the good of the people after it was over - that one's maybe a step too far into the realms of Utopian fantasy. I was so naively happy in my little lockdown bubble at the start of this but reality intrudes, can't be kept out.

I realise I'm not ready for lockdown to end. I'm glad Nicola is being more cautious than Boris. I'm ashamed to admit a tiny part of me thinks a second wave of Covid-19 in London would serve him right; but mostly I imagine how devastated front-line NHS staff, already utterly exhausted, would be if they had to go through it all again.

May 18th to May 25th

No.10 strategist Dominic Cummings
broke lockdown ...

Diabetes linked
to one third of Covid deaths...

Quarantine for
incoming travellers to UK...

Restricted August opening
for Scottish schools...

Rose: **Lockdown Rap**

Hold up, hold on, hold out for change
Now's a chance to rearrange
Turn it up, turn it down, turn around,
We are all standing on common ground.

Locked down in limbo, wrapped in a bubble
Cross the road, we're causing no trouble.
Formal is the new normal, follow the rules
Set out in briefings by tyrants and fools.
I'm feeling the fear, I wish you were here,
Look in the mirror, the future's not clear.
What's up? WhatsApp. Zoom in the room
Breaking up, breakdown, warnings of doom.

Stay in, stay down, stay out, stay home
Hold down, hold up, hold to your own

There is crisis exploitation,
While we clap hands across the nation
Staying safe, keeping our distance,
Lock up, quarantine the resistance.
No justice, no juries, no plaza, no square
Stay at home and grow your hair.
Power to the selfish, the hidden, the clowns
Questions are silenced, democracy shut down
The great recession, a greater depression
This is no time for freedom expression.

Stay up, stay put, stay quiet, stay alert
Roll up, roll on, roll out the experts

Keeping us safe, sanitisation
When what we need is immunisation.
Masking our faces, blame projection
Infection, protection, it's time for reflection
Our borders are closing, the fruit hangs unpicked
Roll up your sleeves and care for our sick.
Elders go to the back of the line
You can go before your time.
Call centre workers like battery hens
No distance, no safety, this could be the end.

Go back to work, revive the nation
The time has come for resuscitation.

Make out, make bread, not making a fuss
Close down, close up, control the virus

Speak up, speak out, write a new page
Stitch a new garment, begin a new age.
The world upside down, no more taking for granted
Gather up, gather round, the seeds have been planted.
Value the carers, the sharers, the workers
Angels and heroes. Who now are the shirkers?
No return to a normal of greed and depletion
We'll make a new order of fair restitution
There's a pot of gold at rainbow's end
Protect life on earth, reach out to a friend.

The world is surviving, the planet can breathe
Life will return, time to grieve.
Sing out, sing round, sing up for sanity
Reach up, reach out to our common humanity.

Acknowledging Kate Tempest: *Hold Your Own*

Beverley: **Lockdowns**

Today would have been my husband's 80th birthday. Thursday is also to be the beginning of the easing of lockdown – so a milestone week. I remember the fantastic party we had in 2010: a joint celebration of my husband's 70th birthday and our youngest daughter's 21st birthday. They chose to share the celebration and have a huge Circus Party. The two of them dressed up as ring masters and everyone else came in circus costume, from dancing bears to hairy fairies. Guests ranged from golden oldies to fashion design students and our grandchildren, and the entertainment included acrobats in a Big Top and a circus workshop before lunch the following day – a party never to be forgotten.

Then my thoughts turn to the last time we were in lockdown. In 2001, due to the Foot and Mouth disease outbreak, we were locked down at Rusko from February 19th to the end of October. As the first case in Dumfries and Galloway was just over three kilometres from our farm, we were locked down for the duration, but not culled. We were not allowed to sell any cattle or sheep, have any visitors to our self-catering holiday accommodation or meet friends, particularly any farming families. In some ways there were similarities to the coronavirus lockdown as people were prohibited from travelling, which meant tourism businesses had no income that year and we didn't see our families. The Forestry Commission closed all the forests in Dumfries and Galloway and no-one was allowed to walk on farm land or in the countryside. Farmers whose stock was culled received compensation. They didn't have to work for the rest of the year and they received grants for tracks and ponds. For those of us who were not culled, not only did we receive no compensation but we had double the amount of stock to feed and look after. Since we were not allowed to sell our animals we received no income. Those of us involved in the tourist industry had a double whammy – a totally income-free year! Most of us struggled to recover from this terrible setback. At least this time there is some aid for some businesses.

Because access to farms was prohibited, we had disinfectant mats on the road; we took on delivering the post to the farms up the valley and collecting the refuse, so as not to risk spreading the infection. If farmers met other people they had to quarantine for a week afterwards. I only did this once when I was invited to a fact-finding meeting with William Hague (then Leader of the Opposition) in Lockerbie. Other than that outing, my husband and I did not see anyone else the whole time.

One of our two stockmen had a stroke right at the beginning of our FMD lockdown, at the beginning of lambing. We wanted to keep our lowland and hill sheep flocks separate, so my husband and I took on the lambing of our 600 lowland sheep – a very steep learning curve. This came to be something we loved doing, so we continued with just one stockman for the next ten years. I especially enjoyed my middle of the night and early morning forays into the lambing sheds, the quiet murmuring of the sheep to their new lambs and being out in the cold, still, starlit nights. We thoroughly enjoyed working the farm together and, strangely, the weather was fine for most of that early spring and summer too, just as it has been so far this year.

The main difference for me has been that this time I have faced lockdown alone and without a purpose and that has made all the difference: from an enjoyable, if worrying, bonding experience to a lonely pointlessness. Perhaps these happy memories have made it all the harder to bear.

Lynn: **The Pain and the Glory**

Paul Tillich, philosopher and theologian, said "Language… has created the word 'loneliness' to express the pain of being alone. And it has created the word 'solitude' to express the glory of being alone." So, today I sit pondering both the glory and the pain. Over the last few weeks I'll admit I have been swithering between the two.

When lockdown first began I was shocked and slightly indignant that my family were instructing, no, ordering me to self-isolate – not because I am frail or have underlying health issues, but because I am old! I didn't realise until then that I was old and/or vulnerable. I could have taken umbrage at the revelation if I didn't recognise that they used the same words I spoke repeatedly when addressing them as they were growing up: "It's for your own good."

It took a while to self-motivate before finally getting stuck into doing some chores around the house. I tackled tasks that I had been putting off for some time. When they were completed, that was the glory. The pain came as days turned into weeks and I began to question the point of expending so much energy when no one would be crossing the threshold to appreciate my efforts anyway.

The pain appears again as day after day I wander round and round the house like a demented hamster in its wheel looking for something I have misplaced. I can't blame anyone else for touching it (whatever it is) and it can't have been stolen because nobody's been in the house for weeks. Considering the fact that I spend all my time these days in only two rooms of the house, except for my nightly expedition to the dining room to pour a richly deserved gin and tonic, there should be no reason in the world that I can't find the blasted item. But oh, when I finally discover that it is still exactly where I left it, the glory comes with the realization that no one was present to witness my folly.

Ah, the pain and the glory.

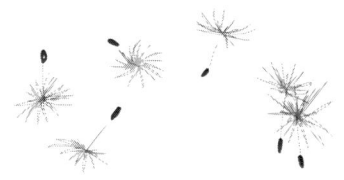

Mags: **Pathway out of Pain**

The gradual ending of isolation has confirmed my sense of apartness so that I don't feel that I can contribute to this project any more. Things will not change for me until I get the spinal treatment I am awaiting and a new hip. My pathway out of pain and weariness involves separate medical departments who do not communicate with each other, despite my GP's best efforts. "It's their turn...no it's your turn." They dispute the exact order of procedures, and anyway, "it's not life-threatening is it?". My lovely daughter has now taken over communications for me and my sense of relief is greater than my feelings of lack of control.

So, you see folks, I cannot be the Moaning Minnie and write any more of my personal situation. Friends and family, distanced by phone and Skype, or lurking naughtily in my garden, well spaced-out when the sun is shining, keep me sane and happy. *Panorama* programmes about refugee camps in Greece make me weep ineffectually. As does awareness of children in deprived families on our own doorstep who suffer by not having the support that school brings to their dysfunctional lives. They can't respond to online educational activities while Facebook-busy mums and dads outbid each other for glory in the home education stakes.

I have good resources in my own tightly-bound little world which is full of love. Yesterday my daughter and I held hands… 'rebel, rebel' comes to mind. Perhaps I should dress in punk attire to complete the picture?

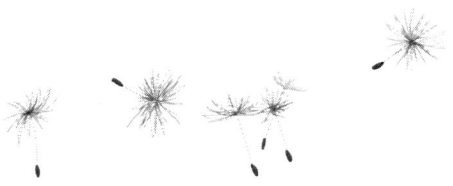

Cath: **Apathy**

I think apathy has set in. This morning, after eight or nine hours sleep, it was a real struggle to open my eyes and force myself to bestir my stumps. Geoff kindly brings me a cup of tea every morning to help me to wake up – otherwise I'd probably stay in bed all day! How do other people manage without this welcome alarm clock?

It is a huge effort to go for a walk which is supposed to do me good. I always feel better when I've been, but starting off doesn't get any easier. Sadly, the bluebells are starting to fade in some of the places I pass. They have been amazing again this year, the restful blue sea under the brilliant green of the canopy of baby leaves completely swamps the senses. It is always a sad moment when this blast of late spring starts to give way to the season ahead. Unfortunately, the beauty of the countryside does nothing to stimulate my enthusiasm for getting on with things.

I despair about the politicians' response to the coronavirus crisis. At first everyone was doing their best to protect people as the situation unfolded. Now, after two and a half months, the thinking seems muddled and illogical. For weeks we were told that wearing masks was unnecessary (despite their use in other countries); now people are advised to wear them in shops or on public transport. The quarantining of travellers has been non-existent, but will start next week! Why? It should have been done months ago. This was discussed ages ago but we've had weeks of shilly-shallying. We are more confused by the day. And don't get me started on the lack of routine testing…

These thoughts and the confusion and mixed messages add to the feeling of helplessness and apathy. I hope other people are not as enfeebled as I am. Many people are starting new projects, running meetings on line, and co-ordinating goodness knows what. Some are running businesses remotely and making deliveries. They are extremely inventive, imaginative, and enthusiastic. Even thinking about it all makes me exhausted! My worry is that I won't feel like doing anything even

129

when things start up again. My get up and go will have got up and gone...

Even the entertainment of 'Eating what's in the freezer' is beginning to pall. Geoff found a parcel labelled 'Two sunk sponges to fill with fruit and cream'. They were only wrapped in greaseproof paper so they were pretty dried out and unappetising. Even the cream and stewed rhubarb didn't help. The second went into a huge trifle; eating it feels more like a duty than a joy. With hindsight, I think next door's hens would have enjoyed them more.

As I've been too lazy to weed the garden, I sit and watch the dandelion clocks disintegrate in the breeze, casting their fluffy seeds out into the world. I wonder where they will land?

Leonie: **Wildlife Garden Journal**

Mid-May and fledglings litter the lawn: sparrows with oversized gapes and quivering wings, dumpy confused-looking blackbirds, screaming sharp-beaked starlings and their overworked parents to-ing and fro-ing, bills hanging with provender.

I left them to it and went for a walk in the woods three minutes from my house. Did I really want to leave my safe place? The first things I found were a puzzle. A ring of plucked feathers looked like the work of a sparrowhawk. One step away lay a ball of soft feathers prettily marked with alternating 'Vs' in cream, caramel and black. A step further away I found a fallen nest of fresh moss lined with white feathers faintly grey-barred.

I couldn't work out if the objects were connected, nor the identity of the nest builder, nor the feather ball. Time to enlist the help of wildlife detectives Mearns and Mearns. From my photos they decided the nest was a chaffinch's and the feathers from a red-legged partridge. We agreed that there was no connection between the nest and the feathers. Later, looking carefully at my photo of the nest, I saw one clearly-marked partridge feather woven into it. I deduced that the nest was built after the partridge was killed.

On the downhill edge of the wood I found my next puzzles. Beside a young hazel grew an enormous tree with a girth of 280cm, which must have pre-dated the community planting. The trunk bore numerous, huge burrs, the bottom branches were dead and curiously distorted. Far above my head its canopy was fresh and green.

I had no idea of the species. Between its roots I discovered, in a single layer, a cache of over 300 discarded cherry stones each with a small round hole. I found a smaller cache of cherry stones mixed with hazel nuts, all with holes. Examining the nuts and stones with my handy x8 lens I could tell from the absence of gnaw-marks that the feaster had been a bank vole. Back home, after consulting Tim Ewing and Google, I could confirm that the grotesque tree is a gean or wild cherry. The bank vole had chosen well.

Margaret: Yellow and Gray

The hill is bright yellow, gorse and broom smelling of coconut. Deep in the wood the kite chicks have hatched at last. The fading bluebells have been trampled by large hooves: one of the dogs startles a red deer - maybe fled from the wildfire? There's been a lot of activity round the badger sett; I should come back by moonlight.

Forced to stay on my own ground, I see it as never before. I've hardly been in a car, and then my farthest goal has been to pick up food at Loch Arthur. Every detail of that journey is a glimpse into a foreign country - horses in a field, a cottage on a hill, a loch seen through trees - there's still this other world out there, outside the Glenkens. Most days I've not been more than two miles from home. I've been dwelling in a world of infinite distance and colour. I'm not sure, now that there's a change in sight, that I actually want to leave.

I used to teach literature - books about other lives, books full of poetry, observation, nature, passion, awareness and colour - in a grey seminar room on the sixth floor of an inner-city tower block. From the north windows we could see the far-off hills, hazy through layers of pollution. I'd walked those ridges. I'd lived intensely in one place, aware of all the other lives in the same small green space. The difficult part was bringing that knowledge back into the grey world where I now found myself. I was there to teach other people how to see things differently. It's hard to change the colours other people see when you're all surrounded by grey fog.

The way we lived caused the danger we are now in. Very few people treated climate change, species extinction, environmental collapse, faraway wars or genocides, or even the untold suffering in the next street, as real emergencies. If you don't want to see the effects of what you do you daren't look too closely at anything. You have to inhabit that grey fog which may make hard truths feel softer, but it also extinguishes colours. It took a pandemic on our doorsteps to galvanise any kind of concerted action. In the face of the emergency that threatens us this very day - not just somebody else, somewhere else - we have all become very obedient and public-spirited. We can't take to the streets to protest. That democratic right is now closed to us - because of the pandemic. That's very convenient for those who have vested interests in business as usual.

I look at footage of Indian families walking hundreds of hot miles to get back to their villages. I see the television reporter take off his shoes and give them to the man who has none. So many stories every day - enormous cruelties and small acts of kindness. I walk in the woods every day and these things drift through my mind like dustmotes and settle somewhere. While that is happening I watch the dogs run ahead in the sunshine. I smell the broom and I smile because it is so very yellow.

Anna: **Mother Nature Fights Back**

Fifty years ago my husband wanted to take me out for dinner on our second date. There was only one restaurant in Edinburgh not associated with a hotel, in a ground floor flat in Abercromby Place. We fell in love across the dinner table, got engaged four weeks later and married ten weeks after that - I suppose one could call it a whirlwind romance but it has lasted almost 50 years now!

At that time the planet was struggling to cope with the overpopulated world. Now the population is at least three times greater and the planet is in freefall. Nature has tried to bring it under control with various viruses, swine flu, bird flu, AIDS, ebola, dengue fever and other epidemics, but clever scientists keep developing vaccines except this time with Covid-19, I fear the virus is winning as it keeps mutating every few days, thus out-manoeuvring the scientists.

Our sleepy-headed politicians just let things continue as normal for too long. Ten weeks later they are considering restricting flights to avert a second wave of infection.

Mother Nature must love their inadequacies. I am very short on hope for the future. I fear that many thousands of people will become unemployed as businesses collapse. Poverty will become the new norm. We will experience anarchy and civil unrest on our streets - perhaps even revolution!

Our Planet Earth accommodates only animals! The human species has proliferated out of control. The human species thinks it will control Covid-19 with yet another vaccine, but people are dying worldwide in their thousands. The planet can no longer sustain the human species in its present population numbers so there will inevitably be spikes and more viruses until this species comes under control.

Why has the human species not learned from the amazing bird population which also occupies this planet? Birds build their little homes in a sustainable manner, raise their young, then fly off to their holiday homes half way round the world, completely self-sufficient and destroying nothing, respecting all that Mother Nature has provided. The same could be said for most of the animal kingdom and the wonderful creatures of the oceans whose very existence is now threatened by the mountains of rubbish and plastic dumped by the human species.

Ann G: **Carrots Galore**

I ordered six carrots with the Sainsbury delivery last week. When the shopping arrived, there were six, large, kilo bags of carrots. As one bag after another emerged, we fell about laughing. A positive mountain of carrots was sitting on our kitchen worktop.

As a result, we now have a serious amount of carrot soup in the fridge. Carrot cake was the obvious other option, but I was already making a large chocolate cake for Bob's birthday. At this point I ran out of options and wrote a big notice saying 'Spare carrots - please help yourself' and put the remaining bags out on the front garden wall. Within an hour, they had all gone to good homes.

The carrots were a welcome distraction from the bigger picture. I find the confusion of lies and half-truths infuriating at the moment. Why will the Westminster politicians in particular never do anything other than assert, with no evidence whatsoever, that they have done a wonderful job?

I read the optimistic bits of news when I can, about green new deals that might follow and how we don't want to go back to the old normal. A welcome bit of positivity caught my eye: a review of *Humankind: A Hopeful History* by Rutger Bregman. I loved reading about the alternative, true-life version of *Lord of the Flies*, which involved co-operation and conflict resolution rather than mayhem and murder. I'm afraid, though, that I don't hold out much hope for greater equality and justice in any future world with Johnson and Trump holding hands across the Atlantic.

This week I've been escaping to a lighter world of excess carrots and birthday cake. We had the now-obligatory Zoom birthday party, with all five families involved. Little party pieces from around the country kept us highly entertained. Then each family lit a birthday candle and, with children primed and ready to blow, Bob magically blew each out in turn. We sang 'Happy Birthday' to the accompaniment of bagpipes.

This silly poem I adapted for the occasion probably illustrates best where my head seems to be at the moment. At least it amused the grandchildren.

The Axolotl and your Grandad
(Adapted from a poem by Catherine Johnson)

> Never give your axolotl chocolotl in a botl
> Serve it in a tiny eggcup, not too cold and not too hotl.
> Make him sip it very slowly, not too much, and not a lotl.
> After all, he's just a tiny, snuggly, friendly, axolotl.
>
> On the other hand your Grandad, he likes chocolotl quite a lotl
> It's better than champagne if you can serve it in a botl
> Cos if he has too much champagne he might just lose the plotl
> He's happy with some orange squash if that is all you've gotl.
>
> His seven years plus seventy is really not a lotl
> When he seems so young and full of fun, his age is hard to spotl
> He walks each day along the prom and goes at quite a trotl
> And what is best, at 5.15 he's Zooming on the dotl.

Gordon: **The Media**

Trying to find something good or reliable on TV or radio makes me ask how have they got into their current state? There's often little actual information content amongst all the chatter and what there is is often misleading. Take basic reporting like corona deaths. Death means death, surely? But no, eventually it is revealed that it was just hospital deaths. They didn't do their homework.

On radio, Radio Scotland seems the worst for meaningless chatter but Radio 4's aggressive *Today* programme is a close second when the facts are what we want, not lots of aggro. And what's the most important news? The weather forecast because it actually affects what we are going to do today. When and where will we go for our exercise? What shall we wear? What can we do in the garden? Will it frost tonight? Radio 4 squeezes it into around a minute for the whole country, sometimes even less so that they can get BBC programme advertising in. Radio Scotland has weather forecasts but the local Dumfries and Galloway forecasters take the weekend off – the very time we (in normal circumstances) need the forecast most!

Budget morning, like so much news reporting, is mostly speculation, which costs almost nothing to produce. All we see is the presenter or reporters talking into a microphone. Do they really have to stand outside Number 10 when the only activity is the rain coming down or the cat looking bored? When we do get interviews with real people, they are often just staged for the reporters to show how clever they are at bullying the interviewees. We're just getting interested in an answer when the interviewer butts in and shunts them off onto a particular hobby horse of theirs. Why can't we have more background? I suppose the answer is obvious, proper background and well reasoned analysis needs research and that costs time, money, patience and an analytical mind. You have to look outside the BBC news programmes, but even there it's getting worse. The newish chair of *Any Questions*, Chris Mason, rambles on, wasting time and pushing the panel members off course just when they are saying something interesting.

As for the newspapers, *The Glenkens Gazette* does a better job than any of them.

Roger: **So -White Galloway**

Listening to today's US news, I recall the summer of 1968. I am resting in the warm sunshine reading about events in the US. Half a century ago I was startled into awareness of absent voices, those not included in the dominant US narrative of becoming a world power.

I am today challenged to reflect on my present feelings, thoughts, experiences and understanding of race. For example my living in so-white Galloway has twice been broken by residence in rural Bangladesh. There I noticed its English language, its colonial buildings, its books, 'our' clothing brands and the position of district commissioner still continued. More personally, I witnessed over many years how on returns to the UK from France, the car belonging to my friend Ulrich from Barbados was always turned over by officials while mine was waved through.

Carol: **I am Afraid**

I am afraid
Of everything the government says
Of all the inaccuracies
The lies
I cannot now believe a single word
So cannot yet be reassured
Nor will I ever be
I'm afraid.

I am afraid
To step outside my safe cocoon
To venture back into the world
To meet my friend for coffee in the town
To hug my neighbour, my family
Or any of the folk I know
And always will be now
I'm afraid.

I am afraid
That we've learnt nothing
That the 'new normal' will just be
The old normal
That litter will be strewn again – already is
That plastics and carbon fuels and waste
And greed and power and inequality
Will plunge the world into destruction yet again.
WE are the plague upon this earth
I'm afraid.

May 25th to June 1st

Dominic Cummings:
no apology for Durham trip...

10th and last
Clap for Carers'...

Test & Protect
goes live in Scotland...

Minnesota police killing of
George Floyd triggers
world-wide protests...

Rose: Singing Together

On Friday morning I wake up with a song going round in my head, a welcome relief from the usual demons of the dawn:

Across the bridge where angels dwell,
Children play.
Close your eyes to fields of wonder,
Close your eyes and dream

These are remnants of an American folk song from the Thursday evening choir on Zoom. How long can we sustain this clunky way of getting together? It's a pale imitation of our community of voice and spirit, sharing space, sharing breath.

We are muted from each other to avoid the anarchy of voices

slightly out of step. Kate leads us through the songs and I sing along, holding my part on my own. I enjoy seeing familiar faces, I feel connected. Singing lifts my spirits. We are learning a song from Commoners Choir: *Singing Together Apart*. They have triumphed over social distancing by each person making a recording which has been woven together into one whole sound, individual faces appearing in patchwork squares on the screen. Is this the way to go?

> *Singing together*
> *When we're together*
> *And singing together apart.*

We break for the 8 o'clock clap. This week is the last one. The end of an era. I bang my dustpan and brush, the one left out front for cleaning off the spiders and cobwebs from the windows. I've finally completed a job started last summer, painting the outside sills that have waited so patiently. Part of my efforts for 'Balmaghie Bright and in Bloom' showing support for each other and NHS/carers/key workers. Across the road, Kirstin and her daughters have laid out beautiful painted stones. Cath's house is festooned with purple, lilac and white bunting. My Nepalese prayer flags, a gift from Kirstin last summer, are released to flutter in the breeze, a beacon to friendship. Times are turning and we can visit in each other's gardens – at last!

Zoom choir resumes. More chat, more singing. We finish with a song from Merry Hell that is our anthem for these times:

> *Rise up, rise up you hopeful men and women*
> *Who might try again*
> *And with one voice your message send*
> *We need each other now.*

Mike: **Zoom Zoom Zoom**

Zoom, Zoom, Zoom,
We're going to the moon.
Zoom, Zoom, Zoom,
We'll be there very soon.

The rhyme takes me back a decade or so, accompanying a very small granddaughter to 'Rhymes and Rhythm' at Halifax Children's Library. The words were part of the mood music of happy early visits. Little did I know that Zoom would come back, to link us again.

Zoom spans generations and continents and embraces everything, we are told, from *sub rosa* flirtation to high finance and government strategy. Its security, allegedly, is dodgy, and no-one knows how many CIA agents and KGB operatives are busy deciphering our family conversations on the unattainability of Tunnocks Caramel Wafers in Giffnock or Yorkshire. (They are nevertheless abundantly available in New Galloway's Community Shop and, with our Post Office still operating, care parcels are regularly dispatched.)

I adopted Zoom reluctantly, my experience with its forerunner, Skype, being an unsatisfactory introduction. Apart from clunky technology, the ambience was more prison visiting than spontaneous chat. I enjoy our family Zoom sessions however, usually with three households, providing everyone with a fourth wall, proscenium style, into other lives. We watch grandchildren exhibiting cooking skills, new lockdown hair cuts and Lego inventiveness - even a Lego cake to celebrate my birthday. When facing boredom my youngest grandchild shows his expertise in varying the background. Look! They are on Golden Gate Bridge. Wow! They are on the Moon! (Zoom, Zoom, Zoom indeed). Another control sparks an alien invasion.

I have yet to deploy these special effects at our regular board meetings on Zoom, as up to 11 of us navigate the community shop and its enterprises through the trials of Covid-19. It would spice up the evening and provide interesting minutes: "The treasurer was reporting on the state of the reserves from a Caribbean beach when she was abducted by aliens."

Zoom, at family and business level, is proving a convenient device in the communications toolbox, useful in the current crisis, but even the most savvy grandchild cannot activate a hug button or launch an empathy app. Nor can business Zooming replicate the spontaneity of the impromptu gathering to solve a problem or chance encounter to spark ideas. If it became the new normal I fear it would come with a sinister price tag. But will anyone listen to me?

Well probably yes, but unfortunately not the people I had intended to have listening.

Lynn: Red Letter Day

For me last Friday was a red-letter day. My dear friend texted me and wrote, 'How about if I come to you this morning for coffee and we sit in the garden?' I replied, 'Perfect! See you when you get here.'

From the time lockdown began she and I had been video calling each other every morning - initially to check if we had made it through the night, and soon it became routine. At first we stayed in our beds chatting about anything and everything, laughing and giggling like teenagers at a sleepover. We agreed that clearing our diaries of appointments and commitments was an unforeseen plus while being incarcerated. The next line of chat became almost obsessional as we revealed what we were baking and cooking and where we were able to get our kitchen supplies as neither of us had family nearby to do our shopping. Between us we discovered greengrocers, dairies and all manner of shops that would supply us with essentials. Moreover, they delivered right to our door!

Before long I realised that I am, in truth, a morning person who prefers jumping up out of bed shortly after waking to one who lolls around under the covers. She on the other hand is happy to take her time getting up and readying herself for the day, so we decided instead that we would start meeting over a mid-morning cup of coffee.

When she strolled around the corner onto the patio she was smiling from ear to ear. It was so lovely to see her. To celebrate our reunion she was laden with all sorts of treats she had purchased while gaily sauntering through the town on her way over, savouring her new-found freedom. She produced her own cup and I poured the coffee (after each of us gave ourselves, instead of each other, a huge hug). We settled down at either end of the table. She reached into her bag and retrieved a punnet, one for each of us, of delicious Scottish strawberries spied while passing the greengrocer's. I provided the double cream in small pots for dipping. She produced a package of fabulous Italian pastries injected with pistachio cream and I laid out a few modest slices of banana loaf. We sat in glorious sunshine, face to face, luxuriating in each other's company, pretending that we were sitting on a marble terrace in the South of France. It was magic.

And on this special day we spoke of many things, but neither of us broached the subject of the as yet unrevealed changes that will soon be upon us, our loved ones, our country and our world.

Thank you, my friend.

June: Easing Lockdown

Once lockdown eases there are two very different prospects for me. If elective surgery resumes with an early slot for me because my op was cancelled hours before it was due, I shall start a new life.

It could be that I need a new knee as well, after limping so long. Or if the masochists in Glasgow decide that, because I am over 80 I should remain in isolation, I can't bear to consider the implications.

Kirkcudbright courts will re-open soon. With a new hip I might get back to my beloved tennis. I shall be able to play with my grandchildren, walk their dogs, roam Arran again. I shall be able to cycle properly, not just lurch on and off and proceed cautiously using my battery on the flat. Oh to be able to walk instead of tottering in a hunched position. To feel balanced again.

With no new hip I could end in a wheelchair, be unable to use my delightful upstairs living area, be unable to live alone.

But whichever way the penny lands for me, I shall feel strange emerging. This has been a cocooned space. Few decisions to make, no diary, no clockwatching, no responsibility apart from not burdening the NHS; no timetable, no standards and deliveries for my needs. A bit like our desert islands. And I don't look in the mirror. Most of us now have strange hair; my neighbours must worry about that odd woman next door lurching about with her hair on end.

So I'm scared for me personally, but looking at the wider picture I can see so many wonderful things that could happen. What enlightenment for New Zealand to move to a four-day week as part of the solution to a dire economic situation; Bryan was keen to take a job there. Going all out for green development could create many jobs and help the climate emergency. Better routes for cyclists and more walking could help keep cars off the road. A basic income for everybody, a fairer tax system and an upper limit on wealth (ha ha!) could move towards greater equality. We have learnt so much in these few short yet long months. Wouldn't it be amazing if we could act on our new knowledge?

Sack Cummings for hypocrisy, vote no confidence in Johnson for dereliction of duty, cancel HS2, the new gas plant, expansion of airports, Brexit and we might recover respect and have some chance of a more sustainable future. There is so much impetus for a better way but will the powerful hold sway?

Gordon: **Mostly Me and Running**

Because of the combination of my improving but not fully recovered leg and the far from recovered world, 'normal' is not in sight. No formal runs, but the organiser of the 86-mile Ridgeway Run in the south of England has organised a clever substitute. Just record 86 miles in instalments during August, anywhere, anyhow you like as long as it's on foot. Totally meaningless I suppose, but somehow the idea is attractive. So, I'll do that when lockdown is over, might even go there to do it. I'll be on my own. I won't be concentrating on getting to the next checkpoint in time or running through the night, instead just enjoying the scenery, the birdsong and the summer weather (well, the signs are good and we can hope), finding little bakeries, rural cafés, tearooms and B&Bs if they haven't all gone bust. And I'll feel good about it environmentally; getting there and back by train and bus if they are running and getting along by foot. Me time!

It's so different there. Here, the Southern Upland Way is little used, varying from good forestry tracks to totally overgrown uneven footpaths, muddy stretches and places where the path disappears altogether and you have to navigate by the guidance poles (if the cattle haven't knocked them over) by compass or the sun. Spectacular, varied, challenging and great when you want to be totally alone.

The Ridgeway is typical of several long distance footpaths in the south. Quite heavily used though not as much as, say, the Derbyshire paths where you sometimes have to queue up to get through narrow bits. The Ridgeway is mostly wide and reasonable walking quality. It's well signposted, varied, with some lovely views and usually not far from refreshments or overnight accommodation.

The Ridgeway Run will be a good way for me to get back to whatever normal we end up in. Then I'll be all set up to campaign to change the world! Get rid of Growth, replace with Satisfaction. Turn off the street lights after midnight. And back to working on our lovely little local footpaths and walled garden.

Gentle runs are getting better and longer. With little traffic and no rush I can hear the birds, see the wavelets on the loch or the mirror-like reflections when the wind drops and wonder at nature; how things have adapted, like the woodpecker I hear with its amazing ability to drill into wood without pulverising its brain. An incredibly ingenious mechanism like so much in the natural world that we're affecting too much and too quickly for it to keep up.

However, we mustn't forget that there are other major threats. There's the possibility of a Carrington Event such as the one in 1859. A what? Not at all like a virus in its action but the effect is widely disruptive. About every 100 years, the sun lets loose a blast of magnetic radiation that can cripple our communication systems. Long distance wiring may burn out, communication satellites fail; IT equipment could crash, as could the financial system, when money and asset transfers cannot be completed. No doubt there is a response plan somewhere in the Cloud – but that'll be wiped out when it's hit!

I'm very much afraid that the new normal will be a difficult normal. That's well explored by others here. I just hope we can avoid the grey fog enveloping us.

Mary: And Then He Went and Spoiled It All

I was quite excited when I started to write this, knowing the First Minister was going to announce her plan for gradually easing lockdown restrictions. The DH was super excited about golf courses opening. Long phone calls and online committee meetings followed to ensure everything was in place to enable social distancing. I was a little miffed at his enthusiasm to go off, leaving me at home alone. Reflecting on this more honestly, I realised I would actually be happy to have a few hours on my own after however many weeks it's been. Even through two closed doors and a flight of stairs his voice booming all day long on the phone to clients ruins my concentration.

I was also looking forward to venturing further afield, revisiting my regular walking places to which I have to drive. I would be able to see my sister. I was happy garden centres would open again. I confess I did break the lockdown rules once. I'd emailed the garden centre with a list of questions, ending with a comment about how frustrating it was not being able to see what he had in stock. He asked if I was self-isolating and if not, would I like to make an appointment to visit – promising no one else would be there and the staff wouldn't come near me. I was giddy with excitement and the air of secretiveness about it. I spent more than I should.

I couldn't help looking askance at scenes of crowded beaches south of the border. I find the idea of being anywhere with so many people pretty ghastly at the best of times. Add the worry of the virus spreading and a second wave of new cases and deaths occurring and I feel doubly anxious. I hoped things would be better managed here and Nicola's 'slowly does it' approach would let us get on top of the virus.

I would never for a moment have believed that eight weeks ago, the prospect of a walk in a different bit of woodland would have made me feel quite so euphoric. And then - and then Dominic Cummings totally ruined it all. I don't think I have ever felt so angry in my life; an anger that will not go away and alongside it utter disgust and despair. I can't write any more.

June: **Is The End in Sight?**

This group has done both navel gazing and ranting, and become more aware of the environment. Living alone, I have also been thinking more: 'where am I meant to be next?' replaced by: 'where will we all be next year?' I don't consider other authors' pieces to be political, rather they ask how we want to live our lives, what sort of a world we want. I believe we should vote for the party best promoting that, rather than how we always voted or worse how our families voted (we had a poor choice last time!). And we need our peck of dirt for a healthy immune system; our bodies are designed for that. Chemical hygiene is wrecking that system, especially for children.

A cynical *Song for Dominic Cummings* by Dillie Keane, which is on YouTube, has the memorable line: 'Say tatty bye to your granny', implying that this crisis is not the result of government bungling but a Cummings plot for a leaner NHS, attractive for sell-off. Aiming for herd immunity should thin us out nicely. My thinking prompted more armchair action. Petitions signed, letters in the paper, to the Council, letters of praise and complaint. I have stopped writing to my MP. My letters are fobbed off with meaningless quotes. I feel disenfranchised being represented by Boris's parrot.

Unable to collect bird food, I found an offer online, 'no mess, no growth'. My photo of a patio deep in mess with sprouting cracks even after three wood pigeons, two doves, a crow and two hedgehogs had eaten what they wanted, produced a refund. I felt guilty, as their mealworms and fat pellets must be producing tubby young blackbirds. But they are shipping three to four thousand bags a week, so that's OK.

Am I about to lose the affection of my Vietnamese daughter-in-law after another rant? She had never come across a seabird cliff. Beguiled by the beauty, with slopes throbbing with thrift and campion, she nevertheless refused to picnic there; seabird voices reminded her of a horror film. I asked son Simon how he could love somebody who disliked seabirds; I told her she needed empathy for creatures that communicate in competition with raging seas and furious wind. She's coming round.

Am I about to lose a friend, ranting about the human-centric attitude to wildlife? I have loved Leonie's empathetic descriptions of wildlife. My friend killed a beetle. "What made you do that?" I asked. "It was flying into my ear". Duh! What makes us think we are superior to wildlife and can get rid of it whenever it irritates us? We need it.

Are we all a bit unhinged? Perhaps I'm 'doing a Cummings' - alienating folk so I can do what I want; I want to stay safe in my cave. Cummings was prominent in the Cambridge Analytica scandal. So who can guess his plots? Are we safe in his hands?

Ann G: **We Can't Turn Our Backs**

What frightens me about moving away from lockdown is that the horrendous levels of inequality in society will be heightened rather than redressed. I don't know where to look for optimism or hope at the moment.

Homeless people have been put up in hotels, but what will happen after this is all over? Boris said he didn't know that families with interim 'leave to remain' are forced into destitution if they lose their jobs. Women trying to escape violent partners with their children don't have enough safe houses to access. Children in families with hopelessly inadequate housing and income suffer dreadfully on every front. The NHS has been deliberately starved for years as part of a calculated strategy of austerity by this government. The pandemic is simply intensifying and highlighting the suffering. And there it is, laid bare for all to see.

I have tried to avoid being too blatantly political in these contributions, but I feel so helplessly angry. All my life I've been a committed socialist and I don't want to live in a society where there are such extremes of 'haves' and 'have-nots'. What is happening is hurting those who are poorest and have fewest resources disproportionately hard. Levels of inequality are increasing on every conceivable measure. I have no faith that this government intends to redress that huge imbalance as we emerge from this crisis.

They duck and weave and lie blatantly at every turn (although we are lucky in Scotland to have more honesty, clarity and intelligent debate). I take solace in reading the commentaries in *The Guardian*, listening to *Channel 4 News*, respecting Emily Maitlis' brilliant grasp on the situation and Andrew Marr's interviewing skills. Despite the dispiriting, tragic and horribly predictable news, there is some comfort in knowing that some others see the world in a similar way.

And yet I can still live in my safe bubble. My life is fine – comfortable and happy. I've had hard times in the past and my children do have various, major struggles in their lives, but by and large, we're very fortunate. I can enjoy watching some of the excellent programmes on television, appreciate the joy of the National Theatre Live offers, delight in hearing my daughters' voices and their tales of the latest grandchildren's doings. We have Zoom meetings on the calendar now and it's fun to talk to friends and family. There's plenty to keep us busy. Bob says this is how he thought retirement would be – plenty of time to laze around and do our own thing.

We are not shut off, however, from knowing about what is happening around us. Nor are we shut off from feeling that we should take some responsibility for it. We are human; we can't turn our backs on the pain others are struggling with.

Tonight, we clap for the NHS staff and other carers, perhaps for the last time. I have to believe it symbolises some solidarity in the face of this dreadful and continuing injustice.

Carol: **For My Son: a poem written in Mental Health Awareness Week**

I don't know where my son is
I don't know if he's dead or alive
Or existing in a nightmare hell
I don't know if he understands this virus
I hope he does
And learns to wash his hands for the first time
In twenty years
I hope he's coped with staying in
Instead of walking the city streets all day
And understands why all the shops are closed
I hope his paranoia hasn't grown
That he's not cowering in terror
Convinced the aliens have landed
And are trying to kill us all
I hope the team that cares for him
Have not been forced to stay away
Leaving him unsupervised
Unmedicated.

Oh god, I wish I knew where he was

June 1st to June 8th

Two Scottish households can meet...

Big crowds at *Black Lives Matter demos...*

Scotland's first day of *zero Covid deaths...*

UK deaths *pass 50,000...*

Christine: **Reach Out**

Is this the end, or the beginning of the end? It should be a time of support for those who have lost loved ones, when people should be thoughtful to others. That is happening, but we are also seeing exhibitions of score-settling and point-scoring. When there has been trauma on a massive scale, do we really need such displays of pettiness, carried out by those who should know better? The families who have loved and lost deserve better than this. Quiet comfort is needed and it is up to all of us who have escaped unharmed from this awful situation to provide it. Loving words and sympathy will not heal a broken heart, but they will reach out to comfort a struggling fellow traveller.

Beverley: Care, Kindness, Co-operation, Culture and Common Sense.

As we near the end of this project, it becomes more difficult to write. Is it because we don't want to let go of a project which has sustained us through this difficult time? Is it because we will miss sharing our deepest thoughts? Or because we can't cope with the new uncertainty after the strict rules we have obeyed for so long? To my dismay, the bit of my brain which deals with remembering diary dates seems to have disappeared.

I want this piece to be optimistic despite my real feelings. So I am not going to dwell on the past or look at the realistic future. I will just look at the positives and where I would like us to go.

We should surely have learnt that we must act together as one world and the great international organisations such as the United Nations, World Trade Organisation, World Health Organisation, G20, need to step up to the mark, so that emergencies of this sort are coped with using international co-operation and sharing of knowledge. This particularly applies to global warming.

Nationally, we need much more co-operation between political parties, local councils etc and a more imaginative and joined up way of problem solving, using the best brains available.

I hope the high status which key workers have earned during lockdown will be retained in the future by the general public and government alike, and that, in years to come, the NHS, teachers, care workers, councils and other core services will be properly funded and appreciated.

We have so missed all the culture, previously taken for granted, and appreciated all the efforts to provide livestreaming online to keep us sane. It is essential that the arts should get the funding they need to survive and return to providing live performances. I realise our history cannot be changed, but it must not be denied. I hope we will value and learn from it.

I have admired the co-operation and enterprise of local businesses, which have done so much to improve the lives of those who have been shielding. They also need to be appreciated and encouraged in the future and I have been incredibly grateful for the care and kindness of friends, acquaintances and strangers.

The whole nation has developed a passion for gardening, regular exercise and enjoyment of the countryside, open spaces and the wildlife which has flourished during this time of lockdown. It is my fervent hope that all this will continue to be appreciated and promoted as life gets back to some sort of normality. Never again will I take for granted the simple pleasure of conversation over a delicious meal or a hug from a dear friend.

I would like to end where I began with the keys to a good life for us all:

Care, Kindness, Co-operation, Culture and Common Sense

Cath: **Venturing Out**

Today, joy of joys, all the people who have been shielding at home for weeks have been told they can go out! Here in Laurieston I have not noticed hordes of people rushing out and blocking the streets. I don't know of many folk in the village who have been under this extreme form of lockdown. Maybe it is more apparent in the larger metropolis of Castle Douglas. All those vulnerable people must be mightily relieved that the world is suddenly now safe and they can flee their prisons. I suspect that most will creep slowly out like snails emerging from their shells, as their common sense dictates.

We are all starting to emerge from our strict constraints as extra facilities open. Last Friday I went to the garden centre. It felt wonderful to go somewhere different and see the gorgeous array of plants and colourful flowers. I bought several trays. It was great to do something normal. However, I was so excited by choosing the plants that I forgot to follow the one-way system and got nearer than two metres to someone in the aisles. The plants were in pots by the front door the same evening. Hopefully, their jolly colours will continue to cheer us up all summer.

I have concerns, as parts of life return to normality. I love going to the theatre and cinema. Locally we have amazing arts centres, theatre, cultural projects and community groups catering for every taste. We have been blessed to have so many enthusiastic people to organise and run them for love, free of charge. Of course they all need funding to be sustainable. Will this necessary money be available in the future?

People may be more cautious about resuming their cultural activities and, with social distancing rules, a lot of the fun and the value of real human contact disappears. With few 'bums on seats' how will enough revenue be generated to keep things going? Music, drama, exhibitions, workshops, classes and more are what make life interesting and fulfilling. Let's hope that this crisis does not sound the death knell for these wonderful activities. It will be a struggle to get things back to their previous level.

Some people will not see this as important, but to me these things are vital. We've had enough of bare essentials. Time to get back to a bit more colour, richness and imagination so that we can blossom again in the company of others. Sitting in a theatre, or being on stage with the drama group is what I crave.

I just want to be there!

Lynn: **The Joy of Shopping**

During lockdown we take our joys where and when we can. It could take the form of Zooming with family and friends, hanging out with grandchildren and playing games, working on jigsaw puzzles, or just snuggling down under the covers at night in the perfect knowledge that it doesn't matter a fig what time you get up in the morning. Oh, all sorts of things and situations we oldies have come to appreciate in our isolation.

And today there is a treat coming to me sometime between 10 am and 6 pm - a grocery delivery! This is a new venture in my life, ordering online. I live fairly close to a major store in town and used to be in the habit of dotting round daily to pick up whatever I wanted. In fact, I referred to the place as 'my corner shop'. I never felt the need to indulge in a weekly expedition.

Now, however, after the van driver deposits numerous recycled bags on the vestibule floor, I think, "Oh my gosh, did I order all that?" While observing social distancing, we've caught up with his thoughts on the latest Covid-19 news. He departs leaving me with my loot to stagger happily through to the kitchen. Each delivery is like a mini Christmas for me because by the time it arrives, I've long forgotten what I've ordered.

"Really? Chocolate – great! And ice cream – yum! Oops – I see I must have forgotten to ask for cabbage. Oh well, no coleslaw this week." Don't tell me you don't have these high-level conversations with yourself – of course you do.

A few weeks back I requested and got a place on the store's vulnerable list, not because I didn't have anyone to do my shopping for me, but mostly because I got sick of sitting up till after midnight attempting to get a delivery slot online. Now I feel quite pampered having my groceries delivered and feel in a bit of a quandary about the situation. I'm enjoying being able to create my shopping list as and when I feel like it, pressing the button and having the order, as if by magic, appear on my doorstep. I'm tempted to carry on in this mode when lockdown is a thing of the past – if I live long enough to experience it. I dream that when that time comes, instead of shopping, I'll be able to share coffees, lunches, cocktails and fabulous long dinners with my family and friends. Oh joy!

Ann G: **I'm All Right Really**

On Saturday morning, we were on our fortnightly Zoom call to my cousins. We've taken to keeping in touch virtually in the meantime and it's great to see familiar faces and hear their news from all around the country – South Wales, Kent, London, Bristol, Nottinghamshire, West Sussex.

We were just beginning to wrap up when my mobile rang showing my daughter's phone number. She lives in Tottenham, a single parent to a nine-year-old boy, cooped up in a small flat. To my surprise it was my grandson's voice on the phone. The stress was clear in his voice, but he spoke clearly, "My Mummy has cut her finger."

Ah – rapid shift from laughing and chatting mode to try-to-stay-calm-in-emergency mode. "OK, sweetheart, has she hurt it badly? Is it bleeding a lot?"

"Yes," he says. "She is crying."

I can hear her then in the background, between sobs, saying "Tell Granny I'm all right really. It's just the shock."

I try to calm his agitation, asking him to fetch her a drink of water. It's going fine until she obviously tries to look at the injury under the tea towel she has wrapped around it and he gets an accidental peek at it and runs, crying hysterically, from the room.

In fact, that helps the situation because she instantly switches to reassuring him which, in turn, calms her down. I'm trying to check out what has happened while scrolling through options in my mind. It's the common stoning-an-avocado story and she has jabbed the point of the knife into the palm of her hand just below her index finger. She can't ask a friend or neighbour to help in this time of Covid-19, nor will a GP surgery be open on a Saturday. Driving to a hospital A & E department would not be a happy option with a damaged hand and an anxious child in tow.

I'm then thinking, "pharmacist maybe", when she sends me a

photograph of the wound (eek!). I can see that this is probably the right answer. A pharmacist will advise, but it looks to me as if steri-strips will do the trick. Grandson has recovered enough to talk to me again and I suggest he needs to get a glass of water for himself as well, as he has had a shock too.

She phones later to report, having secured steri-strips, antiseptic, bandage and reassurance. Following a bit of Googling, she manages the one-handed steri-strip application and bandaging. Thank goodness for pharmacists. They don't often get a mention. Five days later, all seems to be healing. Phew!

And tomorrow is another day.

Anna: A Visit

Last week we received a rare visit from our elder son who has been on lockdown since the end of February and is expecting to travel overseas again in July.

I was amazed at the lengths to which he went to observe social distancing. We had breakfast and lunch on opposite sides of the terrace and he only came into the kitchen for dinner where I had distanced three chairs around our round kitchen table. He slept on our blow-up, occasional bed in the summerhouse. He dug a latrine in the woods and found a comfortable log on which to perch! He swam in the lochs and created a 'spa' bath in the river where it was just warm enough for a dip in the late afternoon.

During his visit, we spotted a hedgehog and a hare and he photographed an elephant moth on my kitchen windowsill.

He came for two days and stayed for six spending an inordinate amount of time on his iphone. Much as I enjoyed his visit, I did remark to my husband that our family had become quite ill-mannered since leaving home!

Having spent most of our lives in Glasgow and Edinburgh, we love our life in Galloway. Not much has changed for us in the last few months except Griersons deliver my butcher meat on a Wednesday, my neighbours do my grocery shop on a Thursday and Fleet Fish deliver on Fridays. I long to take my new car for a drive and a picnic instead of watching it devalue in the carport. On the plus side, I welcome old friends one after the other: the rhododendrons giving way to the azaleas, now joined by the poppies and day lilies; baby fish appearing in the ponds, skirted by blue and white lupins. Our garden has been a labour of love over 38 years starting from scratch and I do so hope someone will be around to care for it after we have gone.

However, I am not sleeping well at night. There are young, nesting birds calling for food from 4 am onwards in the *Hydrangea petiolaris* that climbs up the wall by my bedroom window. We are to blame as we spend a fortune on bird food providing a wildlife oasis within the forest. We had two pairs of woodpeckers. Then the day before yesterday one flew into a summerhouse window at high speed and killed itself outright, followed by another one yesterday, which did the same thing, breaking its neck. Last year we had three generations of red squirrels, but we have only seen the odd one this year. We also have a lonely barn owl calling for a mate. Last year was the first time we had no barn owl chicks and I don't know why.

Gordon: Looking Forward

A few guesses:

There will be a flood of people coming out of lockdown wanting to see friends and relatives. Trains as full as authorities will allow; jammed motorways; footpaths, pavements and cycle routes unusable unless distancing is relaxed or replaced by masks and sanitising. Best bet will be reducing distancing. In any case, rail and bus companies will lose eye-watering amounts of money, while the government plugs the gap with money it hasn't got.

A vaccine is some way off or may never be found.

All the money being printed by government is not matched by production of real goods and services. North Sea oil can't come to the rescue as the oil price is so low that the oil companies may themselves need to be rescued, rather than generating revenue for the chancellor. Property isn't the answer as the market has to sort itself out to fit increased working from home. The new normal will be a house of cards just like the financial boom of a hundred years ago, and just at the time that there is likely to be another spike in the virus and another lockdown.

Most countries will try to get back to the old normal. Some will just crash with horrifying implications for their citizens; Venezuela already has. A few days ago, I would have said that the political situation couldn't get worse, but now it has, with the murder of George Floyd. The US ship of state with Captain Trump at the helm has hit an iceberg and is holed below the water line with the virus blazing down below. Will it sink or will it struggle on, crippled?

Climate change is racing on. We'll get windier, wetter and warmer and will soon pass the point of no return. Years ago I attended a climate-modelling course. The predictions at that time were bad, but fell short of the actual situation now. Much must be spent on mitigation, like flood prevention or managed coastal retreat.

I nearly forgot – we get Brexit in December to add to the fun. We'll be short of border staff – an open invitation to large-scale VAT evasion and other crookery.

Leonie: **Wildlife Garden Journal**

Since the start of lockdown I have been unable to concentrate on the global issues that had been a major preoccupation: climate change, world poverty, rewilding. Inevitably I have focused on the things that matter most, the well-being of family and friends. The endless news of ever-increasing infection rates, hospital admissions, inadequately equipped intensive care units, news of heartbroken families unable to hold the hand of their dying loved one, all led to feelings of total helplessness. Only when I concentrated on the wildlife in my garden, on its beauty and diversity and tried to translate my experience into something I could share, did I recover my hope for the future. Life will go on.

I've been reading *Chasing the Ghost*, the account by the botanist Peter Marren of his journey round Britain to track down fifty rare native plants. He went to Wales in search of two species of *Sorbus* (whitebeam), those lovely trees whose leaf buds, on opening in the spring, look like white candles raised to the sky. Marren was looking for the Least Whitebeam and the Ley's Whitebeam and he did find and identify them, despite their minute and obscure differences.

A couple of things you have to know about the genus *Sorbus* is that different species readily hybridise and, within species, the trees can adapt to a variety of habitats in which they may look very different. Botanists interested in taxonomy get in a bit of a twist about the details and, in the way of scientists, subject plants to measurements and facts, something that can be quantified and create certainty.

In truth, all life is in a constant state of flux. The whitebeam's defined characteristics amount to a snapshot of evolution in action and in the end the best-adapted may settle down into a defined species. The species idea is a somewhat artificial construct. Let's take a holistic view and enjoy the whitebeam's adaptability and variability and not worry too much about the number of lobes in a leaf.

Maybe there is a lesson here for humankind too. We are very

variable and also adaptable. Scientists have endeavoured to categorise us through measurements, to create IQs, classes, races - 'yes and no' categories that divide us. We have to unite in our actions and from lockdown go back into a world that has changed and is in a state of flux. Have we learned what really matters to us and can we carry forward those precious things?

Maybe we should consult the Indigenous Australians who, after all, have survived for 65,000 years and know a thing or two. They discovered how to walk lightly on the Earth.

Hedgerow Walk

A hedgerow bank, undifferentiated.
Engage it with your eye.
Features emerge.
Mind realises separate forms of grasses,
distinguishes hedge parsley from pignut,
this vetch from that vetchling.
Let go their provisional names,
leave them in their perfection.
Walk on.

Ann M: Castles in the Sand

My contributions have been erratic: spasmodic intentions and rummaging, collecting disjointed thoughts with pen and paper, only for an interrupting wind to swirl them back to corners where they huddle among last autumn's leaves.

I've read other contributions with feelings ranging from admiration and amusement to anger and despair. I realise I don't like politics and I am lucky always to have had nature as a close companion.

Talk of lockdown relaxation fills me with fear, coming too soon and risking the demoralising effect of an upsurge of infection, and more deaths. It seems to herald the weakening of togetherness and co-operation and the casting of blame, interviewers puffed up with hindsight, poised to strike with poisoned darts of loaded questioning to bully and bring down their weary adversaries. A scene often depicted in wildlife programmes: hunt to kill. But then it's perhaps a lioness with cubs to feed. These interviewers are human beings, the same species as ourselves.

The impact on the economy has come to the fore. I heard of some types of shops being opened. Restart the economy, provide some employment, get people spending money. Spend, spend. But on what? Where are the foundations for our new economic order?

We've found a liking for more time. For quietness and open roads, a different, simpler pace of life. In fact, more than a liking: a need. Will we want the endless shopping? We've learned to do with less – invent - adapt – repair - reuse. The throw-away society? That's so yesterday. We need to change and the opportunity is there to rebuild an economy on honest foundations.

I see a stretch of beach, the distant sea and endless sand. Some children are marking out the boundary of the castle where they plan to build a massive edifice, with towers and turrets, steps and moat, embellished with shells and a seaweed flag.

They toil all afternoon, then pause to admire what they have made, before shouldering spades and buckets and wending their way home for tea. They turn to wave it good bye before disappearing beyond the dunes.

While they eat their tea, the tide creeps in. Eventually a ripple reaches the moat. Another pushes in. A sand wall slips. More waves inspect, test and attack. Suddenly the castle is surrounded. It melts into the sea, whence it came.

Next low tide there is no sign of all that endeavour. A rippled surface with space for endless dreams to be played out but not the bedrock for our new economy.

June 8th to June 15th

BAME medical staff
twice as likely to die...

Deaths higher in cities
and poor areas...

Face masks to be compulsory
in Scottish shops...

Arrivals in UK
to quarantine...

Ros: **Let Your Garden Grow Fallow**

Let your garden grow fallow for a time

What will grow, will grow
What will die, will die

Now
The treetops skim the sky
To look up at them gives you vertigo
The rooks, who have made their homes in the highest,
swaying branches,
Chatter companionably to one another through the day
And pull off a stately flypast when twilight comes

The weeds
You spent so much time pushing back
Have blossomed into beautiful, trailing exoticisms
They wind their own sweet ways, un-judged and
un-judging, among one another

The delicate imported plants
That you bought with your money
That you cleared space for in your garden
That you coaxed and cajoled into life
Are long gone
Dust to dust, leaves to soil

What is, is
And what isn't, isn't

You drift, in your softly breathing body
Cup of tea in hand
Through the evening garden
Soaking up the depth, the peace, the space
The fallow time has brought

Cath: **Bubbles**

I love bubbles. At our youngest daughter's wedding, the children blew bubbles at the appropriate time during the ceremony, and very pretty they were too. Rainbow colours, so fragile and transient, small and large, floating on the breeze.

We have heard a lot about bubbles recently. Our five-year-old grandson returned to school last week and is being educated in a 'bubble'. A few children and a teacher do everything together and are not allowed to mix, play, or learn with anyone in another 'bubble'. It is cruel to keep small children apart, unable to play normally.

The same for university students. They will live and learn with a group in a 'bubble'. Lectures online, and no meeting with others outside. I can't believe that will suit students, and quite frankly, what is the point? They might as well stay at home and do Open University courses. Madness. College or university is not just about the course but the extracurricular activities, clubs, and other social interaction!

My dear friend is in a tiny bubble in hospital, recovering from a huge operation which she was not expected to survive. She said goodbye to her husband as the ambulance took her away, fully expecting that would be their last moment together. He is also shielding so can't leave the house. Last night their baby granddaughter was born to great joy, but a glimpse through the hospital window is all she can have. Each family in its own bubble. The bubbles protect us, but also trap us.

So what next? People are itching to start travelling: to visit family and friends at last. Our separate bubbles have kept us apart, like those giant plastic 'hamster balls' at activity centres; each person trundling round inside, trying not to bump into anyone else.

One of two things happens to bubbles. They sometimes float away and disappear, or they pop. One by one the shiny cocoons will burst, and leave us exposed to the world and all its dangers once more.

Lynn: **We Are the Winners**

We baby boomers, as our beloved progeny never fail to point out, have had the best of everything: peace, 'sock hops', love-ins, and rock 'n roll, a choice of jobs, our own homes, foreign holidays, a free health service and pensioned retirement, plus many other assorted privileges. Now 2020 is the year that makes us look back in wonder at the life we took for granted.

We all know there are winners and losers in every situation. I defy anyone to say that during our lifetime this hasn't been *the* 'situation of situations'. Those of us who, during lockdown, have been particularly singled out as vulnerable solely because of age, have gone from being independent pensioners to being forced to confront our own mortality.

Our situation has also given us time, silence and space to meditate on our past good fortune and observe those things that we have possibly overlooked or ignored in our rush to get wherever it is we thought we were headed. We've had time to prioritise just what's important in our lives. Those of us who are lucky enough to have special friends and families - whether near or far - have felt the pain of separation and the anxiety of not knowing when we'll be able to embrace them once more. Although this is definitely a downside, we can anticipate the joy we will experience when we have the opportunity to be reunited again.

Being apart is a trial, but one positive aspect most of us have learned is an appreciation of the wonder of our natural world. We listen to the breathtaking sound of songbirds performing the rites of spring as they have always done. With traffic at a minimum, the surrounding silence has magnified their music and made us realise how exquisite it is, how blessed we are to be here to appreciate it. No matter what's going on in our world, nature carries on regardless; the grass continues to grow, flowers bloom, and trees sway in the wind. Last week I stood looking from a window watching two fledgling blue tits who fluttered from one fragile perch to another. They were excited, surprised to be airborne, and I too was excited. My hope was that they would survive the hunters skulking amongst the ferns. Would I have taken the opportunity to observe them another time? Perhaps.

We must concentrate on the positives, and as the song goes, eliminate the negatives. We know beyond a doubt that life will change. And in the words of W.B.Yeats, "If what I say resonates with you, it is merely because we are both branches on the same tree."

Roger: Hamilton Road, Rutherglen

Perhaps lockdown has brought us a new reason for use of this path, though historic Rutherglen has a wide main street with a 17th-century church, and magnificent 19th-century library, Town Hall and Post Office. A bookshop here might flourish. Takeaways are plentiful and so is the choice of pubs. Lockdown has mobilised quite a flow of people of all ages and mobilities along the path throughout the day. This is a community without obvious social differentiation but what's clear is the common struggle to deal with the present national circumstances. My local paper reports council backing for an initiative supporting the victims of domestic violence during lockdown.

I hugely value the freedom to move about in an urban environment after the negative experiences I associate with Galloway: access laws are one thing, landowner behaviour something else entirely. Indeed nowhere else walking in the UK have I experienced so many nasty encounters with class attitudes. Sometimes it's patronising, like being asked, "You will close the gates, won't you boys?"

As a Rutherglen outsider I observe the community. When I walk on the path there are acknowledgements and exchanges between folk by name. Clapping on Thursdays, everyone participates on both sides of the road.

Evening runners are common. Voices outside are normal, small children holding a hand as they chatter on with family. Older people who struggle with mobility pass more slowly. Community exists. A hairdresser came to our back garden for my cut under the sun, so needed in the lockdown.

Oh, the pleasure.

Katy: **Ebb and Flow**

My spirits ebb and flow like the tide. At my lowest, I feel stuck. Chores remain neglected and I struggle to motivate myself to work. I miss my colleagues and the buzz of our building. I miss my family and our raucous conversations. There is too much time to reckon with my own mind; questions swirl until I am felled by uncertainty and doubt. About where we will live, my career, children, lockdown, deaths, the economy. I have an idea for the future, but it seems so far away. We don't know where August will see us, but the city calls like a siren and we will not resist.

Then new life comes to us in the form of a tiny and hairy nephew. My heart lifts and when we phone my sister-in-law, we can hear him gurgling in the background, content and sleepy. His parents name him Jimmy and it is a good name; I call my brother the same and he is gentle and conscientious. Carefully, I cut the letters of his new name out of mountboard, dampen some paper and run the letters through rollers so that they leave an imprint. I add some inked newborn legs and post it to his parents. It is the closest I can come to a ceremony.

And then our screens are filled with violence and hatred. I watch the Black Lives Matter protests unfurl and feel sick at how deep the roots of institutional racism go. I recall my dissertation on the thousands of black volunteers from the West Indies who served in the Second World War. They grew up singing the National Anthem and believed that Britain would welcome them. But even today, our government questions their right to be here. We accepted them as labourers, but not as neighbours. A discussion with my family leaves me dismayed; I cannot understand how they have so much to say about statues being torn down and so little about George Floyd or Breonna Taylor or Ahmaud Arbery. I feel guilty for not doing more.

The tide flows and at my highest, I am thankful for my privilege. The here and now is my focus and I take time to read, move my body, be creative. One Sunday evening, I prepare dinner, drag my husband from his revision, and take him to a small loch. The fishermen have left; we have only the insects and birds to share this peace with. The water makes our bodies tingle and our breathing short. Above us, a swallow darts through the air. We drink in our joy. Later, our hands turn white as we cycle home, but it hardly matters – we are healthy and free and surrounded by beauty.

The tide comes and goes and I try not to wrestle with it.

Margaret: **The Faceless Ones**

1955. A child is wheeled into the operating theatre. The lights are too bright. The people have no faces.

The man is angry: "Why is this child still awake?"

She thinks it's her fault. A man clamps something hard over her nose and mouth. She can't breathe. She fights back. For 30 seconds maybe. Then she's out.

Even now, I'm afraid of people with no faces. I'm afraid of masks. Of having my nose and mouth covered. Of not being able to breathe.

Just born, you take your first breaths and you see: forehead, nose, mouth, eyes in the right place, which meet yours. You already knew; you expected that.

A child in a strange, noisy, hard place, full of kids you don't know, you look for a face. That's the teacher. Her mouth smiles. You take a deep breath. That's better.

You meet your friend. The café's full of faces. People's eyes meet; their mouths keep moving as they eat and drink and talk. Maybe you were sad when you sat down, but soon you feel happier.

The face at the checkout is stony; you unload your shopping quickly. The face breaks into a wrinkly smile and says, "Lovely weather for the time of year." You leave with a lighter heart.

The crowd is full of faces. Each face is full of stories. Some faces are young, some old. Some are black, some brown, some white. Some are women, some are men. Some subvert all oppositions. This is the world going by. You could watch the faces all day and every single one would be different. You could spend the the rest of your life watching these wonderful faces. This is the breath of human life.

This one - with the freckles and bright eyes

This one - with the wide embracing smile

This one - with the lines of a long-lived life

This one - with skin like a peach and no front teeth

Imagine a world without faces. Where people wear masks all the time. How will they see one another? How will they treat each other? How will they learn to care?

The people whose faces you don't know all seem pretty much alike. The ones who are just statistics on a screen. Their numbers overwhelm you. If they're not your people, it's hard to imagine them with faces anyway. Actually it would be easier not to hear about them at all.

Suppose you're making vital decisions about 68 million or so people, nearly all of whom, as far as you're concerned, have no faces? Would you give a toss what happened to each one of them? Really?

I'm afraid of masks.

"I can't breathe."

"All the same to me. I am your murderer. The way I see you, you have no face."

Ann G: **Rollercoaster Days**

We're going through photographs and I have a great boxful. This is one of our most daunting sorting tasks, but one we can take time over. Now in our mid-seventies, we each have a lifetime of memories to look back on. A photograph can hold a moment in time. "It takes me back." Such a hackneyed phrase but what depths it carries.

I can gaze at myself as a baby and feel my mother's arms. I see my father with the camera – click – that winter of 1946 when the snow reached the windowsills of my grandparents' house in Aberdeen and a path was dug to the washing line to hang out my nappies. And here, I remember the sun on my five-year-old skin as I cavorted naked in the garden of my other grandparents' house in Hayling Island. There are my school friends and I am transported back to them. Click - now I am graduating. And my children – oh my children! So small they were, and so dependent on my less-than-adequate care. How precarious it seems now, looking back, to bring up children. And yet they grew, so strong and brave and beautiful. My heart swells.

I inhabit these places and spaces in my mind, re-live the feelings, see again the houses I have lived in, the journeys I have made, relationships made and broken, those I have loved and lost. I'm launched into a space-and-time warp and no longer know who, where or what I am, might have been, or am becoming. I'm exhausted by it as well as exhilarated. It's a rollercoaster of delights and sorrows.

These days of Covid are an emotional rollercoaster too. Everything is more intense, feelings more exaggerated. I cry so easily, whether happy or sad tears, seems hard to say sometimes. No matter where I look, everything seems to have a greater significance than before. There is a heightened level of threat. Each lens yields a picture that is so loud in its import, it screams out for our attention; demands our very presence.

Click - The test, track and trace system will be allegedly 'world-beating' - except that it's barely functioning yet!

Click – 50 per cent of deaths have occurred in care homes!

Click - At least twice as many Black and ethnic minority citizens are dying, but the special report is redacted to say no more than that!

Click - The chief executive officer of SERCO is chortling that the latest contracts secure their takeover of our public health services!

Click - A policeman in America murders a helpless Black man with three colleagues looking on!

Click - A fifth of households with children are now going hungry!

Click - Trump poses with the Bible in his hand!

I'm deafened by the volume and intensity of these cries. But equally powerful and intense are the messages of hope and positivity that bombard me too. Communities are coming together to support each other. Volunteers and organisations are pulling out all the stops to ensure people are fed. The kindness of strangers makes me weep. I ache to watch the sacrifices of those who keep working in health and social care, in pharmacies, on buses, in shops and delivery services to give us what we need and want; risking their own lives for others. Too often losing their lives.

I inhabit these places and spaces in turn, relentlessly tossed this way and that, from one extreme to another. Where are we heading? What time-frame are we occupying? Is this the future now, or a repeat of yesterday? What will we become?

Mary: **Reach Out and Touch**

I've spent the last however many weeks ricocheting between a state of fury, incomprehension at how this can have come to be, and despair at how social and economic inequalities have been so sharply revealed and will be ignored by those in power. It's exhausting.

I listen to Boris Johnson saying he is 'proud' of how the pandemic has been controlled and wonder what planet he's living on. The UK has achieved the highest death rate in Europe. Has no one made him aware of this? Some scientists are saying thousands of deaths could have been prevented if lockdown had been put in place sooner (hadn't most of us already worked that out? And how does it make grieving families feel?). Our economy is set to suffer greater damage from Covid-19 than our neighbours in Europe. Oh, yes, and there's Brexit. It sounds like post-lockdown we're going to be up shit creek without a paddle – with Boris at the helm.

And I have an earworm. You know when a song plays relentlessly over and over in your head and you can't shift it? It's usually only a couple of lines rather than the whole song, which makes it even more annoying. Two songs in particular afflict me – I only need to read the title, even without actually hearing them play on the radio: *The Lord of the Dance*, and *Two Little Boys* by Rolf Harris. Either one of them is enough to make me want someone to slice off the top of my head and scoop out the relevant bit of brain.

But the earworm I've had for the past few days hasn't had such an extreme effect. Instead, the beautiful voice of Diana Ross inside my head makes me so unutterably sad, tears keep welling up.

Reach out and touch
Somebody's hand
Make this world a better place
If you can.

Those words have never felt so meaningful and so poignant. It's what we all need right now. The touch of someone's hand on ours would make the world seem a better place. Such a simple gesture and yet, many weeks ago, we allowed ourselves to be frightened into excising a huge part of our humanity, to keep ourselves and others safe. My heart breaks seeing young children file into their classrooms, keeping the regulation six feet apart, learning they mustn't touch or hug each other. Learning to be fearful of their friends and their teachers. This, at a time when we are most in need of the comfort the touch of another human brings – a hand on our arm, a quick hug, a pat on the back, a hand reaching out to touch our hand.

June: Finale

It feels as though many of us are holding our breath, as if we have reached a tipping point. Will we get a new surge in cases or was the easing of lockdown well-timed? Will we move to new, more sustainable ways of doing things or will we revert to big business?

Covid-19 has had a massive impact on everybody. Last week I was 84. This week I put away my winter clothes, took out my summer clothes and got a shock. These were young peoples' clothes. Sleeveless tops, short skirts, low-ish necklines and several pairs of shorts. Last year, even throughout the winter, I was toned and brown. This year, after my cancelled operation, I am flabby, white and bow-legged: not a good look in shorts. Lack of strenuous exercise has so many ill-effects; less oxygen so poor energy; memory loss, poor decisions and, combined with lockdown, loss of confidence and a resistance to trying new things like Zoom. I feel half the person I was. But it's shaming to care so much about such things when I think about the dead, the hungry, the battered, the mentally ill, the homeless, the jobless, young people with their hopes cut short, the exhausted NHS and other key workers.

Yet huge numbers are braving the virus to march for a better deal for Black, Asian and minority ethnic people. There's an ongoing fight for the NHS. Throughout the world there's agitation for action on the climate emergency. Extinction Rebellion and many more have joined the fight to prevent wiping out a large proportion of wildlife. Cities are working to reduce air pollution. Even banks and business leaders are campaigning for a better way of doing things. There's an exciting momentum for creative ideas.

Today my garden is full of sunshine, flowers, my best roses ever, myriad shades of green sparkle, and everywhere baby birds being fed by their tattered parents. I've beaten the birds to two strawberries and eaten my first black kale. The salad is ready, the apple trees laden, vegetables growing tall and soft fruit ready to ripen. What a stunning world we share. Can we learn to cosset it? Or are we who care doomed to be, as in the recent *Observer* cartoon, the ragged crew, saplings in hand, facing the belching beasts of big business?

Anna: Seventy Years Back, Seventy Years Hence

70 years ago we lived in a prefab, single glazing, no central heating, no pollution, little traffic and very few aeroplanes. We either walked or travelled to school by tramcar.

70 years ago there was no such thing as plastic. Now this non-compostable product litters the oceans, beaches and kills marine life in the oceans.

70 years ago we took holidays on the Ayrshire coast or travelled as far as Rothesay or Millport. Now we travel to the furthest ends of the earth by plane and cruise liner.

70 years ago, our carbon footprint was negligible, now it is out of control.

70 years ago, there was food rationing but no starvation, now the 20 per cent of humans who live in developed nations waste enough food to feed the 80 per cent who are starving. There is enough food in the world; we just don't have the infrastructure or political desire to spread it around.

70 years ago, we had rain forests which captured our carbon

waste, now these are being destroyed for food production and greed.

Now we need to save our planet and tackle climate change. Or...

70 years hence, there will be no polar ice.

70 years hence, with sea levels having risen more than a metre, all low lying countries will no longer exist.

70 years hence a billion people will have headed to Northern Europe to escape the overheating of the equatorial regions.

70 years hence, there will be little or no drinking water.

70 years hence, mankind may no longer exist.

70 years hence, the animal kingdom will have evolved and once again inherit the earth.

My hope is that I am wrong but the science all politicians seem to rely on these days, says I am not!

Cathy: **Where are we now?**

Weary

Fed up

Can't complain

Alive.

Get deliveries

Freezer, fridge, and cupboards stocked

Community functioning

Not bored

Plenty to do

But fed up

And angry

The drama, the horror, the sacrifice, the tragedies, have slid into a morass of political sludge, slimy wrigglings, lack of honesty, weasel words (why do we denigrate weasels?) incomprehensible amounts of money, huge changes in the world of big business, frightening side effects, autocratic behaviour and shocking figures.

We've done our bit. Change.

Big things may have to change. Very big things.

It's OK to admit bad decisions, it's OK to admit bad history. Some things are history and some things are responsibility.

Life is complicated.

Admitting and apologising is simple.

A first step.

And then.

Action.

We are going to be in a Covid world for a while yet -
Take the long view
Act.
Change
for the better.

Rose: **They're Back!**

I hear voices outside the front window.

"Look, there's that stone I painted."

"I painted that one."

The scrunch of gravel down the side of the house as Ruby and Edie run down the garden. Theo comes to the back door.

"Hello Theo, how nice to see you. You look hot in your penguin onesy."

"I'm in camouflage from Ross and Bruce. Rose, can we go in your shed?"

"Yes you can, thanks for asking. Just take your shoes off when you go inside. And Ruby, second rule is to leave it as you found it."

"Can we get some blankets and cushions? Let's make a house. Come on everyone, I know where there's some pillows, in the spare room."

"We don't have a spare room, it's the sleepover room, but I guess it's spare at the moment."

"I want to see my bed, I can't remember what it looks like. Is our den still there? Ruby! Ruby, our den's still alive, the one we made with Ali and Iona."

They play, they fall out. Theo wanders round the garden, swinging at things with a hammer, banging on stones and posts. Ruby stands at the back door like a well behaved stranger observing lockdown etiquette, "Please can I use your toilet?"

The afternoon ends, cutched up on the couch, watching *Peter Rabbit*, laughing together. Just like the good old days.

But it's not the same. The familiar is unfamiliar. When I go to the doctor's, the waiting room is stripped bare – no leaflets, no magazines. Chairs carefully placed apart like desert islands on a sea of red carpet. Outside the chemists, masked up, we distance queue.

There are things that can't be undone. The criminal negligence of the deaths in care homes. The beaches of the world we knew littered with debris after the storm. Chlorinated chicken emerging through the political smokescreen, winging its way to our shores. The coronavirus veil is drawn back and the ugly truth that lies behind is revealed, the votes cast, the deals done.

Time fades so fast as lockdown eases. Have I dreamt it all, frozen in time and space, one day melting seamlessly into the next? I used to tell Ruby adventure stories about a little girl who sailed to magical islands. She would always come home safe, to wake up wondering if it had all been a dream. But no, a feather or a petal in the adventuring bag under her bed, would prove she'd really been there. As I emerge slowly from my lockdown cocoon, the pages of our shared writing are there, under my bed, reminding me of where I've been, what we've lost and what we've found.

Mike: **Back to 'Normalcy'**

One hundred years ago this summer Warren G Harding was set on running for president. Capitalising on post-war exhaustion and pioneering a Republican tradition of mangling the language, he promised a return to 'normalcy'.

A journalist coined the phrase 'smoke-filled rooms' to describe the shady power-broking cabals of the 1920 convention which selected Harding. With his promise of 'normalcy' he won the presidency by a landslide. He went on to betray the war veterans who had supported him, presided over the bizarrely-named 'Teapot Dome' scandal - the worst in American history until Watergate - and Nan Britton, his mistress, added to his legacy with America's first political 'kiss and tell' memoir. For a century Harding has been a front runner in the league table of America's 'worst ever president' (until 2016 that is). So much for the 'normalcy' the weary voters of 1920 had longed for.

So what might the 'new normal' look like for the weary pandemic survivors in Britain? Our hopes have been raised for a more relaxed and caring society, a world more aware of the values of community, the importance of the environment, and a humane life and work balance.

But while lockdown is relaxed, we are certainly not. From Dorset's Jurassic coast to the shores of our own Loch Ken we have witnessed aggressive invasions of urban vandals, displaying no respect for local people or their environment. Weeks of grim city lockdown appear to have brewed a toxic resentment of the 'lucky' countryside, threatening to add an urban/rural tension as yet another fault line in our fractured society.

The clear skies of our locked down world are disappearing as the new normal sees the return of the car as a safer option than public transport, while fear of car-sharing multiplies the traffic. The labour force, required to expand and get the economy moving again, will be bolstered by the return of 'shielded' workers now being 'liberated' from protection.

Lockdown may soon disappear but Covid-19 will not. Much of 'normal' life is not returning any time soon. If ever. What of the spontaneous carefree meal out or drink in café or pub with friends, the visit to cinema or concert, the fellowship of choir or band; what of worshippers or hobbyists and sports people meeting one another? And what of young people at school, college or university, fed a digitally packaged diet of information but stripped of the holistic education of growing up and learning in a society with one's peers. The regimes planned for the 'new normal' bear meagre resemblance to the normal we crave.

And what of the freedoms we surrendered, supposedly temporarily? How do we demonstrate against the new austerity? What a relief for the government, returning to 'normal' policies, that the lingering menace of Covid can be used to curb climate change campaigners and keep environmental protestors off the streets. How very very convenient.

And if you are tempted to defy the restrictions and join that demonstration, just remember the phone in your pocket. Smart phone it may be but not so smart to carry it. Invaluable of course for tracing your Covid contacts but anyone else deemed 'a person of interest' will be in the net as well. With unconscious candour Americans call their mobiles 'cell' phones. It's been observed that Orwell accurately foresaw the state craving ever more control of the individual. He failed to foresee citizens complicit in their own monitoring.

Welcome to 'normalcy'.

Frances: **Back to the Surface**

Down here on the seabed, my sunken wreck, weighted down by leaden limbs, holds on - just by breathing. Far above me, in daylight, someone is snoring.

I must prompt myself to eat and drink. My body offers no signals to remind me. I get up and do it, mechanically, then crumple back down and sprawl. Nothing moves down in the seabed twilight until eventually my bladder provokes me.

For five weeks I am here alone with Covid. Thank goodness I don't have to account for anyone else. That would demand too much.

When those electric, chest clamping spasms come – the signature I recognise for my Covid – I am afraid: is this time the last, am I going to die now? Or can I get hold of help? Or am I any good at deciding when help is needed? (That hospital doctor said only when your pain is 8 out of 10 or above. What number am I at today? Am I just making a fuss?). I am most fearful at night-times and weekends, when I can't call on the reassurance of a calm and professional GP at the end of the phone.

I have no cough, no fever, at any time. I always have to explain why I think I have the virus. Eventually, I have a test which returns positive. Three weeks after that, my GP reckons I am not infectious. Lindi and Ken move in. I feel overwhelmed at their bounteous kindness, their love and care and sensitivity. And because I feel less alone, less vulnerable, less frightened. Less reliant solely on my own, dubious, evaluation of my own health.

Gradually I come to the realisation that I am not just a day or two away from being my normal self; I am no nearer to doing all those lockdown tasks I had optimistically listed. Articles appear in the press describing what one writer calls 'long tail' Covid: there is a growing cohort of people who do not recover in a couple of weeks, but have debilitating symptoms carrying on... for how long? We don't know, as we are the first. The symptoms still strike at random, and often with ferocity: this virus is a snake in the grass.

I have let go completely of the creativity that was formerly the engine of my days. I have disconnected myself from long-standing groups and activities. I cannot bring myself to read the other mass observation contributions. Somehow there has not been space in my brain for other people's stories, nor for the news, my intake of which I minimise – just enough to follow the main points, enough to feel disgust at our government's cynical and inept handling of this disaster.

For days on end the sun shines. On my birthday, Lindi and Ken bought me a reclining chair. I recline in it and consider empty space.

Upstairs there are voices – serious, urgent, engaged – talking across continents, time-zones, languages, while I lie down here, a blob, struggling to connect thoughts, to stick with a book for more than three pages at a time, sinking yet again into exhausted sleep. But I *am* dressed, as on every day since this started; while they – hard at work – sport PJ bottoms and at best a presentable top.

My nails need cutting. Again. I only did them five minutes ago. This is my new measure of time.

I am improving. I have energy to cook, most days. I can spend all waking hours thinking about what to make. I have planted veg and potted up plants, doing a little bit at a time.

Good friends stay in touch, with emails, texts and phone calls. I am touched by kindnesses from unexpected quarters. I get to know my neighbours, chatting across garden boundaries.

I read, over the course of a week, all the contributions for this book, and feel moved by the wealth and breadth of experiences which have been motivating people to write all this time.

George Floyd is murdered, and there is sorrow and anger in my house; at this outrage, and at all the others that have preceded it. We know there is a continuum between them and the racist behaviour which Ken and Lindi have experienced here, in Castle Douglas. They each find positive ways in which to further an anti-racist discourse; they inspire me out of my lethargy to write about racism myself.

Having done which, I know I can write a final piece, as requested, for this book.

Carol: **Coming Out Of Lockdown**

No!
No!
This is not the end
This is a false security
We are not done with it.
I will no longer listen
To inconsequential ramblings
From a government guilty
Of lies and double standards
Of culpable homicide.
My rage, subdued and silenced by my lockdown fears,
Has now returned as smouldering fire
Yet more each day
It feels an ineffectual stance
Ignored by those whose role it is
To keep us safe.

No, this is not the end!

Biographies

Ann Glaister grew up in Aberdeen, then worked down south as a child psychologist in the health service and later with the Open University. Lots of writing involved, but she has enjoyed other forms of writing since retiring and moving back to Scotland. She loves being a mother and grandmother.

Ann Maxwell grew up on a Norfolk farm. She taught in Rhodesia; after marriage, she and John were posted to Kasungu, Nyasaland: a steep learning curve on African crops, and growing children! In 1964 they settled in Galloway, with family, sheep and cattle. Working with nature has always been important.

Anna Blyth, 49 years married with three children and four grandchildren counts gardening, upholstery, sewing, painting and now writing amongst her interests. Having experienced homelessness in Glasgow as a child, leaving school at 16, hard work was fundamental to her success as sales director for a national catering company.

Beverley Vaux, born in Kent, grew up in Rio de Janeiro. She was educated in England where reading and writing were her favourite occupations. Life then got in the way; secretarial college, working, marriage and children, charity work, farming and a tourism business. She now enjoys writing in retirement.

Carol Salsbury has lived in the Glenkens since 1998, having escaped the city in order to live closer to her ethical beliefs. She is passionate about wildlife, and her love of gardening reflects this. She is best known as one half of the Wyrdy Women, an acapella folk duo.

Cath Monk moved to Laurieston from Berkshire 21 years ago with her family. She loves the range of cultural and artistic activities on offer locally. She is a member of Crossmichael Drama Club, and enjoys sewing and art. She has five children and seven grandchildren living in Scotland, England and France.

Cathy Kinnear is a slighty scatty retired planner/art teacher living in Fife. Originally visiting friends who had moved to New Galloway, she has become a lover of the area with respect and admiration for the community and its activities. She's untidy, doesn't do ironing, and loves wild places.

Christine Rae, born in Somerset in 1950, moved to Kippford aged 5, then in 1960 to Dalry. She trained as a speech therapist and worked in Galloway. Christine produced many plays and performed in local pantomimes. She inherited her father's love of words, lulled happily to sleep by his stories.

Frances Hlanze is 68, white, tallish, retired and retiring. She lives alone with a ground source heat pump so lockdown in the colder months was comfortable. After retiring from work Frances was enjoying playing at being creative but that game stalled during Covid. Frances hopes for that to change soon.

Gordon Hill is a retired database designer and a long distance runner. His writing is influenced by time in Africa in the early 70s, then in Europe and back in the UK. His fiction, which he expects to publish soon, explores major themes like the future of humanity.

June Nelson, an elderly, outdoor person, enjoys reading, writing, sport, gardening, culture and animal watching. After travelling widely, as Bryan's field assistant, she appreciates difference. Above all, she hates the havoc wrought by people, and the chasm between 'haves and have-nots', longing for a fairer world in harmony with its environment.

Katy Billington, at the time of writing these entries, lived in Dumfries and Galloway and worked in youth arts, both of which she loved. She enjoys biking of all kinds, reading whatever she can get her hands on, and dabbling in various arts and crafts, especially printmaking.

Leonie Ewing, retired biologist and farmer with a lifelong interest in natural history, likes all forms of writing especially poetry. She combines walking and photography in Dumfries and Galloway to inspire her work.

Lynn Otty grew up on the Canadian prairies but now has spent the majority of her years living in Dumfries and Galloway. She writes a bit, loves films, her friends and her family of three children and four grandchildren. She also loves travel and is always up for an adventure.

Mags Glencross was born in Dalbeattie in April 1945. Many lives, a wonderful daughter and son, and two equally lovely grandchildren later, she returned to her roots six years ago. Glasgow was her early midlife haven, Galloway her retreat as old age approached...stealthy as ever! Now, words are her world.

Margaret Elphinstone first moved to Galloway in 1984 and is here for the duration. She has published novels, essays, poetry and literary criticism. She taught literature at university, and has run writing groups for thirty years. She lives in New Galloway with Mike, and has two daughters and five grandchildren.

Mary Smith is a Dumfries & Galloway-based writer of fiction, non-fiction including local history and memoir, and poetry. From Castle Douglas she ventured south of the border before extending her horizons to Pakistan then Afghanistan, a country which still keeps her in its clutches despite being back home for years.

Mike Brown left school in Edinburgh hoping for a life in journalism and the countryside. After 40 urban years in media he achieved his second goal. He now lives with Margaret in New Galloway, walking, writing, singing, sawing, gardening and watching advancing wind farms and Sitka spruce.

Pam Swift moved here last November to take up ministry at St. Margaret's Episcopal Church. She has previously served in Possilpark, Glasgow and in London, Leeds, Newcastle and Liverpool but has also lived on Skye, Hadrian's Wall and the Yorkshire Dales. Her entire family consists of Penny (collie) and Koshca (cat).

Roger Adams, born Wales 1945.11+ Rutland, Oakham School 1957. 1962 moved 5th form to Cheltenham Grammar School. Universities: London, B Sc; Wales, MA; Lancaster, MPhil. Social Work CQSW 1972/ 2003. Voluntary Sector. Then 2003/4 VSO Bangladesh. Has walked in Spain, Sweden, Palestine, Germany. Left Galloway in 2018 for Glasgow.

Ros Elphinstone first became resident in Dumfries and Galloway when she was 11 years old. Her various life experiences have led her to pursue a career in counselling and psychotherapy. She has three daughters.

Rose Ardron moved to Laurieston four years ago after over 40 years living and working in inner-city Sheffield. She wanted to be closer to family and to enjoy the natural beauty of Galloway. She loves to sing and to swim, having been a mermaid in a former life.

The writers reflect:

Although we were never able to meet as a group, we built a strong community through our shared e-mails:

We supported and encouraged each other as writers, and more:

"I do enjoy your writing and it comes over loud and clear that you are enjoying it too - I find your enthusiasm quite infectious. Your piece on food has started me thinking. Thanks for all your insights."

"All the sad stories are coming out now, after a few weeks, maybe it's getting to us at last. It's not easy to stay as upbeat as we were at the start. And we're all missing the contact and the hugs. This is to all who have written about difficult days. At least we know 'it's not just me.'"

"Truly wonderful. Says so much, so sparingly, and precisely. I felt every word to be an echo of my feelings."

"I shall tell you something, we have become a close-knit supportive group and it is lovely to be part of it all."

Sometimes we laughed – and sometimes we cried:

"I haven't met you but I love your sense of humour! This was a great contribution at this depressing time and made me laugh out loud…! Carrots to you too!"

"Thanks for your piece. Just what we all needed I thought. A laugh, some good political thoughts and a delightful poem. Perfect."

"Lovely. I was smiling throughout reading your piece. We've come to appreciate small things."

"I loved your piece. So much of what I read in these pieces brings tears to my eyes, just because it's real and catches me as so apt and sensitive-ly done."

It became a safe space where we could be honest and vulnerable:

"Thanks so much for your emails. Your words let me have a wee cry. Last night I couldn't, so thank you for that. A good greet can be quite healing. I was so glad of the group, simply to be able to put in writing what had happened and send it off."

"A difficult one for me to write, but I felt that honest self-examination was the only way to go."

"I just loved this. A litany of all the ills of the world, including your own pains, and then that truly wonderful last paragraph. Your magical last sentence brings me to tears every time I read it."

Our views of the wider world were diverse – we ranted, questioned and listened:

"Your words are uncomfortably true. Thank you for voicing them."

"You've tipped me into trying to find ways to connect with and influence the world as we emerge into it, however much we may want to shout at it!"

"Your words, experiences of coronavirus have, more than anything else, aroused me to the reality and nearness of this endemic plague, shattering the so-called security bubble."

"I've loved everyone's contributions, some happy, some sad. All thought-provoking."

"Here is my final piece. It's been quite a ride."

We found it hard to let go:

"I shall miss this splendid project."

"I'm missing it already! It's hard to put into words (!) what a special and important part of my lockdown days it's become."

"Me too - I'm going to miss the new contributions coming in, and all the comments that follow. It's been quite a dialogue. I hope contacts have been made that don't have to stop now."